CATHOLIC PRAYERS

". . . All things whatsoever you shall ask in prayer, believing, you shall receive."

—Matthew 21:22

Congratulations!
A Confirmation Keepsake
St. Mary, Our Lady of the Snows
April 17, 2016
Archbishop Allen H. Vigneron

The Blessed Virgin Mary in adoration and prayer before
the Child Jesus, with Angels in attendance.

CATHOLIC PRAYERS

Compiled From Traditional Sources

By

Thomas A. Nelson

"If you abide in me and my words abide in you, you shall ask whatever you will, and it shall be done unto you."
—John 15:7

TAN Books
An Imprint of Saint Benedict Press, LLC
Charlotte, North Carolina

Imprimatur: Rev. Msgr. David D. Kagan, J.C.L.
Vicar General
Rockford, Illinois
July 3, 2007

ISBN: 978-0-89555-595-3

Cover illustration and frontispiece: Painting by Heinrich Kaiser (1813-1900); photo by Victoria Ambrosetti. Photo © 2007 TAN Books and Publishers, Inc.

Printed and bound in the United States of America.

TAN Books
An Imprint of Saint Benedict Press, LLC
Charlotte, North Carolina
2013

Dedicated to
The Blessed Virgin Mary,
Our Model in Prayer

Some Notes On Prayer

Prayer is "a raising of the mind and heart to God." Prayer is made for four basic reasons: 1) to *adore and praise God*, 2) to *thank Him* for blessings received, 3) to *ask pardon for* and *expiate* (or "make up for") *our sins*, and 4) to *petition Him* for all our needs. To be effective, prayer must be 1) *humble*, 2) *confident*, 3) *persevering*, 4) *focused* (not wilfully distracted) and 5) *penitent* (with sorrow for our sins). There are two types of prayer, *mental* and *vocal*. Mental prayer is meditation on spiritual truths; vocal prayer consists of repeating set words. All vocal prayer has some mental prayer built in. *Catholic Prayers* is a book of vocal prayer. St. Anthony Mary Claret (1807-1870) found vocal prayer much easier than mental prayer and felt Our Lord's sensible presence more in vocal prayer;[1] he became so holy that toward the end of his life he received the grace that the Blessed Sacrament was always conserved in his breast.[2]

Everyone is obliged to pray, for without prayer—as St. Alphonsus teaches—we shall not receive the actual graces necessary to save our souls. We must ask for them.[3] We cannot say, "God knows what I need; I don't need to remind Him!" Rather, Scripture admonishes us, "in everything, by prayer and supplication, with thanksgiving, let your petitions be made known to God." (*Phil.* 4:6). The Saints concur with St. John Chrysostom (347-407) that "It is simply impossible, without prayer, to lead a virtuous life."[4] Therefore, we should "Pray without ceasing." (*1 Thess.* 5:17).

---

1. *The Autobiography of St. Anthony Mary Claret,* Louis Joseph Moore, C.M.F., Trans., 1945; TAN, 1985, p. 197.   2. *Ibid.,* pp. 180, 181.
3. St. A. de Liguori, *The Great Means of Salvation and Perfection,* Part I, Ch. I, Sec. I.
4. Cf. *Voice of the Saints,* Sel. & Arr. by Francis W. Johnston, 1965; rpt. TAN, 1986, p. 35.

Table of Contents

— Part One —
BELOVED PRAYERS

— **Part Three** —
FAVORITE PRAYERS

— Part Four —
SPECIAL PRAYERS

"Offer to God the sacrifice of praise [the Mass], *and pay thy vows to the most High. And call upon me in the day of trouble, and I will deliver thee, and thou shalt glorify me."* (Psalm 49:14-15).

"Let nothing hinder thee from praying always, and be not afraid to be justified even to death, for the reward of God continueth forever." (Ecclesiasticus 18:22).

"Watch ye, therefore, praying at all times, that you may be accounted worthy to escape all these things that are to come, and to stand before the Son of man." (Luke 21:36).

"Ask and it shall be given to you; seek and you shall find; knock and it shall be opened to you. For everyone that asketh, receiveth; and he that seeketh, findeth; and to him that knocketh, it shall be opened." (Matthew 7:7-8).

"If two of you shall consent upon earth, concerning anything whatsoever they shall ask, it shall be done to them by my Father in heaven. * *For where there are two or three gathered together in my name, there am I in the midst of them."* (Matthew 18:19-20).

---

*This promise depends, of course, on the persons fulfilling the five requirements for effective prayer. (See page vi in this book.)

The Sign of the Cross

This most fundamental prayer is used to begin and end one's prayers and to ward off the attacks of the devil. It is especially powerful when used with Holy Water.

IN THE NAME of the Father, and of the Son, and of the Holy Ghost. Amen.

Our Father

OUR FATHER, Who art in Heaven, hallowed be Thy Name. Thy kingdom come, Thy will be done on earth as it is in Heaven. Give us this day our daily bread, and forgive us our trespasses, as we forgive those who trespass against us. And lead us not into temptation, but deliver us from evil. Amen.

Hail Mary

HAIL MARY, full of grace, the Lord is with thee; blessed art thou among women, and blessed is the fruit of thy womb, Jesus. Holy Mary, Mother of God, pray for us sinners, now and at the hour of our death. Amen.

1

Glory Be

GLORY BE to the Father, and to the Son, and to the Holy Ghost. As it was in the beginning, is now, and ever shall be, world without end. Amen.

The Apostles' Creed

I BELIEVE in God, the Father Almighty, Creator of heaven and earth; and in Jesus Christ, His only Son, Our Lord; Who was conceived by the Holy Ghost, born of the Virgin Mary, suffered under Pontius Pilate, was crucified, died, and was buried. He descended into Hell; the third day He arose again from the dead; He ascended into Heaven, sitteth at the right hand of God, the Father Almighty; from thence He shall come to judge the living and the dead. I believe in the Holy Ghost, the Holy Catholic Church, the Communion of Saints, the forgiveness of sins, the Resurrection of the Body, and life everlasting. Amen.

The Act of Faith

O MY GOD, I firmly believe that Thou art one God in Three Divine Persons: the Father, the Son and the Holy Ghost. I believe that Thy Divine Son became man, and died for our sins, and that He shall come to judge the living and the dead. I believe these and all the truths which the Holy Catholic Church teaches, because Thou hast revealed them, Who canst neither deceive nor be deceived.

The Act of Hope

O MY GOD, relying on Thy almighty power and infinite mercy and promises, I hope to obtain pardon of my sins, the help of Thy grace, and life everlasting, through the merits of Jesus Christ, my Lord and Redeemer.

The Act of Charity

O MY GOD, I love Thee above all things, with my whole heart and soul, because Thou art all-good and worthy of all love. I love my neighbor as myself for the love of Thee. I forgive all who have injured me, and ask pardon of all whom I have injured.

The Act of Contrition

It is good to begin our prayers by purifying our souls with an act of contrition.

O MY GOD, I am heartily sorry for having offended Thee, and I detest all my sins because I dread the loss of Heaven and the pains of Hell; but most of all, because they offend Thee, my God, Who art all good and deserving of all my love. I firmly resolve, with the help of Thy grace, to confess my sins, to do penance and to amend my life. Amen.

The Confiteor

I CONFESS to Almighty God, to Blessed Mary ever virgin, to Blessed Michael the Archangel, to Blessed John the Baptist, to the holy Apostles Peter and Paul, and to all the Saints, that I have sinned exceedingly, in thought, word and deed; through my fault, through my fault, through my most grievous fault. Therefore I beseech Blessed Mary ever virgin, Blessed Michael the Archangel, Blessed John the Baptist, the holy Apostles Peter and Paul and all the Saints, to pray to the Lord our God for me.

May Almighty God have mercy upon us, forgive us our sins and bring us to everlasting life. Amen.

May the Almighty and Merciful Lord grant us pardon, absolution and remission of all our sins. Amen.

The Hail, Holy Queen
Salve Regina

HAIL, holy Queen, Mother of mercy, our life, our sweetness and our hope! To thee do we cry, poor banished children of Eve. To thee do we send up our sighs, mourning and weeping in this valley of tears. Turn then, Most Gracious Advocate, thine eyes of mercy toward us. And after this our exile, show unto us the blessed Fruit of thy womb, Jesus. O clement, O loving, O sweet Virgin Mary.

V. Pray for us, O holy Mother of God.
R. *That we may be made worthy of the promises of Christ.*

The Memorare
Famous Prayer of St. Bernard of Clairvaux

REMEMBER, O most gracious Virgin Mary, that never was it known that anyone who fled to thy protection, implored thy help or sought thy intercession was left unaided. Inspired with this confidence, I fly unto thee, O Virgin of virgins, my Mother.

To thee do I come, before thee I stand, sinful and sorrowful. O Mother of the Word Incarnate, despise not my petitions, but in thy mercy hear and answer me. Amen.

Prayer After the Rosary

O GOD, Whose only-begotten Son, by His life, death and Resurrection, has purchased for us the rewards of eternal salvation, grant, we beseech Thee, that meditating upon these Mysteries of the Most Holy Rosary of the Blessed Virgin Mary, we may both imitate what they contain and obtain what they promise. Through the same Christ Our Lord. Amen.

Prayer to St. Michael
The Archangel

ST. MICHAEL the Archangel, defend us in the battle; be our safeguard against the wickedness and snares of the devil. May God rebuke him, we humbly pray, and do thou, O Prince of the heavenly host, by the power of God, cast into Hell Satan and all the other evil spirits who prowl about the world seeking the ruin and destruction of souls. Amen.

Most Sacred Heart of Jesus

Most Sacred Heart of Jesus,
Have mercy on us.
Most Sacred Heart of Jesus,
Have mercy on us.
Most Sacred Heart of Jesus,
Have mercy on us.

Come, Holy Ghost

V. Come, Holy Ghost, fill the hearts of Thy faithful;

R. *And kindle in them the fire of Thy love.*

V. Send forth Thy Spirit, and they shall be created;

R. *And Thou shalt renew the face of the earth.*

Let Us Pray

O God, Who hast instructed the hearts of the Faithful by the light of the Holy Ghost, grant we beseech Thee, that by the gift of the same Spirit we may be always truly wise and ever rejoice in His consolation, through Christ Our Lord. Amen.

Morning Offering
Of the Apostleship of Prayer

O JESUS, through the Immaculate Heart of Mary, I offer Thee all my prayers, works, joys and sufferings of this day for all the intentions of Thy Sacred Heart, in union with the Holy Sacrifice of the Mass throughout the world, in reparation for all my sins, for the intentions of all our associates, and in particular for the special intentions of our Holy Father for this month. Amen.

Angel of God

A NGEL of God, my guardian dear,
To whom God's love commits me here,
Ever this day (night), be at my side,
To light and guard, to rule and guide. Amen.

Another Morning Offering
Based on Our Lady of Fatima's requests

O JESUS, through the Immaculate Heart of Mary, I offer Thee all my prayers, works, joys and sufferings and all that this day may bring: for the love of Thee, for the conversion of sinners, and in reparation for the sins committed against the Sacred

Heart of Jesus and the Immaculate Heart of Mary. Amen.

Grace Before Meals
(Make the Sign of the Cross.)

BLESS US, O Lord, and these Thy gifts which we are about to receive from Thy bounty, through Christ Our Lord. Amen.

(Make the Sign of the Cross.)

Grace After Meals
(Make the Sign of the Cross.)

WE GIVE Thee thanks, Almighty God, for these and all Thy benefits, Who livest and reignest forever. Amen. And may the souls of the Faithful departed, through the mercy of God, rest in peace. Amen.

ETERNAL REST grant unto them, O Lord, and let perpetual light shine upon them. May the souls of all the Faithful departed, through the mercy of God, rest in peace. Amen.

(Make the Sign of the Cross.)

The Angelus

The Angelus is traditionally prayed standing, in the morning (6:00 a.m.), at noon and in the evening (6:00 p.m.) throughout the year, except during Paschal Time (Easter Sunday through the Saturday after Pentecost), when the Regina Coeli is prayed instead.

V. The Angel of the Lord declared unto Mary.

R. *And she conceived of the Holy Ghost.*
Hail Mary . . .

V. Behold the handmaid of the Lord.

R. *Be it done unto me according to thy word.*
Hail Mary . . .

V. And the Word was made Flesh.
(*Genuflect.*)

R. *And dwelt among us.* (*Arise.*)
Huil Mary . . .

V. Pray for us, O holy Mother of God.

R. *That we may be made worthy of the promises of Christ.*

Let Us Pray

Pour forth, we beseech Thee, O Lord, Thy grace into our hearts, that we to whom the Incarnation of Christ, Thy Son, was made known by the message of an angel, may by His Passion and Cross be brought to the glory of His Resurrection. Through the same Christ Our Lord. Amen.

The Regina Coeli

This prayer is traditionally prayed standing, in the morning (6:00 a.m.), at noon and in the evening (6:00 p.m.), during Paschal Time (from Easter through the evening of the Saturday after Pentecost) instead of The Angelus.

V. Queen of Heaven, rejoice. Alleluia.
R. *For He whom thou wast worthy to bear. Alleluia.*
V. Has risen as He said. Alleluia.
R. *Pray for us to God. Alleluia.*
V. Rejoice and be glad, O Virgin Mary. Alleluia.
R. *For the Lord is truly risen. Alleluia.*

Let Us Pray

O God, Who by the Resurrection of Thy Son, Our Lord Jesus Christ, hast been pleased to give joy to the whole world, grant, we beseech Thee, that through the intercession of the Blessed Virgin Mary, His Mother, we may attain the joys of eternal life. Through the same Christ Our Lord. Amen.

O Sacrament Most Holy

O SACRAMENT most holy,
O Sacrament divine!
All praise and all thanksgiving
Be every moment Thine!

Jesus, Mary and Joseph

JESUS, Mary and Joseph, I give Thee my heart and my soul.

Jesus, Mary and Joseph, assist me in my last agony.

Jesus, Mary and Joseph, may I breathe forth my soul in peace with Thee.

O My Jesus

To be said after the Glory Be, *following each decade of the Rosary. This brief prayer was requested by Our Lady of Fatima in 1917.*

O MY JESUS, forgive us our sins, save us from the fires of Hell, lead all souls to Heaven, especially those who are most in need of Thy mercy.

Sacrifice Prayer

Our Lady of Fatima said: Sacrifice yourselves for sinners, and say many times, especially whenever you make some sacrifice:

O MY JESUS, I offer this for love of Thee, for the conversion of sinners, and in reparation for sins committed against the Immaculate Heart of Mary.

The Golden Arrow

To be said in reparation for blasphemy and the profanation of Sunday, revealed by Our Lord to Sister Mary of St. Peter, O.C.D. (1816-1848) at Tours, France, but which may also be said for any pressing need. This prayer delightfully "wounds" the Heart of Jesus, which then pours forth torrents of graces for the conversion of sinners. The Golden Arrow is actually only the first of these prayers, but all said together are extremely powerful.

MAY the most holy, most sacred, most adorable, most incomprehensible and ineffable Name of God be forever praised, blessed, loved, adored and glorified, in Heaven, on earth, and under the earth, by all the creatures of God, and by the Sacred Heart of Our Lord Jesus Christ in the Most Holy Sacrament of the Altar. Amen.

(Pray the above two times).

O LORD Jesus Christ, in presenting ourselves before Thine adorable Face to ask of Thee the graces of which we stand in greatest need, we beseech Thee, above all, to grant us that interior disposition of never refusing at any time to do what Thou requirest of us by Thy holy commandments and divine inspirations. Amen.

13

O GOOD Jesus, Who hast said, "Ask and you shall receive, seek and you shall find, knock and it shall be opened unto you," grant us, O Lord, that faith which obtains all, or supply in us what may be deficient; grant us, by the pure effect of Thy charity, and for Thine eternal glory, the graces which we need and which we look for from Thine infinite mercy. Amen.

BE merciful to us, O my God, and reject not our prayers, when amid our afflictions, we call upon Thy Holy Name and seek with love and confidence Thine adorable Face. Amen.

O ALMIGHTY and Eternal God, look upon the Face of Thy Son Jesus. We present It to Thee with confidence, to implore Thy pardon. The All-Merciful Advocate opens His mouth to plead our cause; hearken to His cries, behold His tears, O God, and through His infinite merits, hearken to Him when He intercedes for us poor miserable sinners. Amen.

A DORABLE Face of my Jesus, my only love, my light and my life, grant that I may know Thee, love Thee and serve Thee alone, that I may live with Thee, of Thee, by Thee and for Thee. Amen.

ETERNAL Father, I offer Thee the adorable Face of Thy Beloved Son, for the honor and glory of Thy Name, for the conversion of sinners and for the salvation of the dying.

O DIVINE Jesus, through Thy Face and Name, save us. Our hope is in the virtue of Thy Holy Name! Amen.

Promises of Our Lord Jesus Christ to Sr. Mary of St. Peter, Discalced Carmelite Nun of Tours, France, to those who thus honor His Holy Face:

1. All those who honor My Face in a spirit of reparation will, by so doing, perform the office of the pious Veronica. According to the care they take in making reparation to My Face, disfigured by blasphemers, so will I take care of their souls, which have been disfigured by sin. My Face is the seal of the Divinity, which has the virtue of reproducing in souls the image of God. 2. Those who by words, prayers or writing defend My cause in this Work of Reparation I will defend before My Father, and will give them My Kingdom. 3. By offering My Face to My Eternal Father, nothing will be refused, and the conversion of many sinners will be obtained. 4. By My Holy Face, they will work wonders, appease the anger of God and draw down mercy on sinners. 5. As in a kingdom they can procure all that is desired with a coin stamped with the King's effigy, so in the Kingdom of Heaven they will obtain all they desire with the precious coin of My Holy Face. 6. Those who on earth contemplate the wounds of My Face shall in Heaven behold it radiant with glory. 7. They will receive in their souls a bright and con-

stant irradiation of My Divinity, that by their likeness to My Face they shall shine with particular splendor in Heaven. 8. I will defend them, I will preserve them and I assure them of Final Perseverance.

Powerful Novena Prayer
To The Infant Jesus
For Cases of Urgent Need

In cases of great urgency, a novena of nine hours may be made instead of nine days. The prayers should, if possible, be repeated at the same part of the hour, every hour for nine consecutive hours.

O JESUS, Who hast said, "Ask and you shall receive, seek and you shall find, knock and it shall be opened unto you," through the intercession of Mary, Thy most holy Mother, I knock, I seek, I ask that my prayer will bc granted. (*Mention your request.*)

O JESUS, Who hast said, "All that you ask of the Father in My Name He will grant you," through the intercession of Mary, Thy most holy Mother, I humbly and urgently ask Thy Father in Thy Name that my prayer will be granted. (*Mention your request.*)

O JESUS, Who hast said, "Heaven and earth shall pass away, but My word shall not pass away," through the intercession of Mary, Thy most holy Mother, I feel

confident that my prayer will be granted.
(*Mention your request.*)

(Then pray the following prayer of thanksgiving.)

Prayer of Thanksgiving
To The Infant Jesus

I prostrate myself before Thy holy image,
O most gracious Infant Jesus, to offer Thee
my most fervent thanks for the blessings
Thou hast bestowed upon me. I shall inces-
santly praise Thine ineffable mercy and
confess that Thou alone art my God, my
Helper and my Protector. Henceforth my
entire confidence shall be placed in Thee!
Everywhere I shall proclaim aloud Thy
mercy and generosity, so that Thy great love
and the great deeds which Thou dost perform through this miraculous image may be
acknowledged by all. May devotion to Thy
Holy Infancy increase more and more in the
hearts of all Christians, and may all who
experience Thine assistance persevere with
me in showing unceasing gratitude to Thy
most holy infancy, to which be praise and
glory forever. Amen.

Powerful Novena to the Sacred Heart of Jesus—A Favorite Of Padre Pio

Padre Pio recited this novena prayer every day for all those who requested his prayers.

O MY JESUS, Thou hast said: "Truly I say to you, ask and it will be given you, seek and you will find, knock and it will be opened to you." Behold I knock, I seek, and I ask for the grace of *(Here name your request).*
Our Father, Hail Mary, Glory Be.

Sacred Heart of Jesus, I place all my trust in Thee.

O MY JESUS, Thou hast said: "Truly I say to you, if you ask anything of the Father in My name, He will give it to you." Behold, in Thy name, I ask the Father for the grace of *(Here name your request).*
Our Father, Hail Mary, Glory Be.

Sacred Heart of Jesus, I place all my trust in Thee.

O MY JESUS, Thou hast said: "Truly I say to you, Heaven and earth shall pass away, but My words shall not pass away." Encouraged by Thy infallible words,

I now ask for the grace of *(Here name your request).*

Our Father, Hail Mary, Glory Be.

Sacred Heart of Jesus, I place all my trust in Thee.

Let Us Pray

O Sacred Heart of Jesus, for Whom it is impossible not to have compassion on the afflicted, have pity on us miserable sinners and grant us the grace which we ask of Thee, through the Sorrowful and Immaculate Heart of Mary, Thy tender Mother and ours.

Hail, Holy Queen . . .

St. Joseph, foster father of Jesus, pray for us.

Pour Forth Thy Grace

POUR forth, we beseech Thee, O Lord, Thy grace into our hearts, that we to whom the Incarnation of Christ Thy Son was made known by the message of an Angel, may by His Passion and Cross be brought to the glory of His Resurrection, through the same Christ Our Lord. Amen.

Novena Prayer to
Our Lady of Good Remedy
Source of Unfailing Help

This is an extremely powerful prayer! Devotion to Our Lady of Good Remedy originated in the 12th century when large sums of money were needed to ransom Christians who had been captured and sold into slavery by the Mohammedans. Under Our Lady's patronage, St. John of Matha and the Trinitarian Order were able to raise the funds to free many thousands of Christians.

O QUEEN OF HEAVEN and earth, Most Holy Virgin, we venerate thee. Thou art the beloved Daughter of the Most High God, the chosen Mother of the Incarnate Word, the Immaculate Spouse of the Holy Spirit, the Sacred Vessel of the Most Holy Trinity.

O Mother of the Divine Redeemer, who under the title of Our Lady of Good Remedy comes to the aid of all who call upon thee, extend thy maternal protection to us. We depend on thee, Dear Mother, as helpless and needy children depend on a tender and caring mother. *Hail Mary . . .*

O LADY of Good Remedy, source of unfailing help, grant that we may draw from thy treasury of graces in our time of need.

Touch the hearts of sinners, that they may seek reconciliation and forgiveness. Bring comfort to the afflicted and the lonely; help the poor and the hopeless; aid the sick and the suffering. May they be healed in body and strengthened in spirit to endure their sufferings with patient resignation and Christian fortitude. *Hail Mary . . .*

D EAR Lady of Good Remedy, source of unfailing help, thy compassionate heart knows a remedy for every affliction and misery we encounter in life. Help me with thy prayers and intercession to find a remedy for my problems and needs, especially for . . . *(Here mention your special intentions).*

On my part, O loving Mother, I pledge myself to a more intensely Christian lifestyle, to a more careful observance of the laws of God, to be more conscientious in fulfilling the obligations of my state in life, and to strive to be a source of healing in this broken world of ours. *Hail Mary . . .*

D EAR Lady of Good Remedy, be ever present to me, and through thy intercession, may I enjoy health of body and peace of mind, and grow stronger in the faith and in the love of thy Son, Jesus. *Hail Mary . . .*

V. Pray for us, O Holy Mother of Good Remedy,
R. *That we may deepen our dedication to thy Son, and make the world alive with His Spirit. Amen.*

Memorare to St. Joseph

This is an extremely powerful prayer that can be said for any need, since St. Joseph is the Universal Patron.

REMEMBER, O most illustrious Patriarch St. Joseph, on the testimony of St. Teresa, thy devoted client, never has it been heard that anyone who invoked thy protection or sought thy mediation has not obtained relief. In this confidence I come before thee, my loving protector, chaste spouse of Mary, foster-father of the Saviour of men and dispenser of the treasures of His Sacred Heart. Despise not my earnest prayer, but graciously hear and obtain my petition. *(Here mention your request.)*

Let Us Pray

O God, Who by Thine ineffable Providence didst vouchsafe to choose Blessed Joseph to be the spouse of Thy most holy Mother, grant, we beseech Thee, that he whom we venerate as our protector on earth may be our intercessor in Heaven, Who livest and reignest forever and ever. Amen.

St. Joseph, Patron of a Happy Death, pray for us.

Prayer to St. Joseph
To Obtain a Special Favor

O BLESSED Saint Joseph, tender-hearted father, faithful guardian of Jesus, chaste spouse of the Mother of God, we pray and beseech thee to offer to God the Father His Divine Son, bathed in blood on the cross for sinners, and through the thrice-holy Name of Jesus, obtain for us from the Eternal Father the favor we implore. *(Here mention your intention.)*

Appease the Divine anger so justly inflamed by our crimes; beg of Jesus mercy for thy children. Amid the splendors of eternity, forget not the sorrows of those who suffer, those who pray, those who weep. Stay the Almighty arm which smites us, that by thy prayers and those of thy most holy spouse, the Heart of Jesus may be moved to pity and to pardon. Amen.

St. Joseph, pray for us.

Prayer to St. Joseph
In a Difficult Problem

O GLORIOUS St. Joseph, thou who hast the power to render possible even things which are considered impossible, come to our aid in our present trouble and distress. Take this important and difficult affair under thy particular protection, that it may end happily. (*Name your request.*)

O dear St. Joseph, all our confidence is placed in thee. Let it not be said that we have invoked thee in vain, and since thou art so powerful with Jesus and Mary, show that thy goodness equals thy power. Amen.

St. Joseph, friend of the Sacred Heart, pray for us.

An Ancient Prayer To St. Joseph

O ST. JOSEPH, whose protection is so great, so strong, so prompt before the throne of God, I place in thee all my interests and desires.

O St. Joseph, assist me by thy powerful intercession and obtain for me all spiritual blessings through thy foster Son, Jesus Christ Our Lord, so that, having engaged here below thy heavenly power, I may offer thee my thanksgiving and homage.

O St. Joseph, I never weary contemplating thee, and Jesus asleep in thine arms. I dare not approach while He reposes near thy heart. Press Him in my name and kiss His fine head for me, and ask Him to return the kiss when I draw my dying breath.

St. Joseph, Patron of departing souls, pray for me.

Publisher's Note: We reproduce here, without comment or guarantee, the following statement which usually accompanies the foregoing prayer:

This prayer was found in the fiftieth year of Our Lord and Saviour Jesus Christ. In 1505 it was sent from the Pope to Emperor Charles V when he was going into battle. Whoever shall read this prayer or hear it or keep it about himself shall never die a sudden death or be drowned, nor shall poison take effect on him—neither shall he fall into the hands of the enemy or be burned in any fire or be over-powered in battle.

Say for nine mornings for anything you may desire. It has never been known to fail.

Prayer to St. Anne
For a Special Need

O GLORIOUS ST. ANNE—filled with compassion for those who invoke thee and with love for those who suffer—heavily ladened with the weight of my troubles, I cast myself at thy feet and humbly beg of thee to take under thy special protection the present affair which I recommend to thee. (*State your petition.*)

Deign to commend it to thy daughter, the Blessed Virgin Mary, and lay it before the throne of Jesus, so that He may bring it to a happy conclusion. Cease not to intercede for me until my request is granted. Above all, obtain for me the grace of one day beholding my God face to face, and with thee and Mary and all the Saints, of praising and blessing Him for all eternity.

O Good St. Anne, mother of her who is our Life, our Sweetness and our Hope, pray to her for us, and obtain our request. Amen. (*Pray this last paragraph 3 times.*)

I thank thee, dear St. Anne.

Prayer to St. Jude
Patron of "Hopeless Cases"

O GLORIOUS APOSTLE St. Jude, faithful servant and friend of Jesus, the name of the traitor who delivered thy beloved Master into the hands of His enemies has caused thee to be forgotten by many, but the Church honors and invokes thee universally as the Patron of Hopeless Cases, of things almost despaired of. Pray for me who am so helpless and alone. Make use, I implore thee, of that particular privilege granted to thee to bring visible and speedy help where help was almost despaired of. Come to my assistance in this great need, that I will receive the consolation and succor of Heaven in all my necessities, tribulations and sufferings, but in particular, that . . . *(here make your intention)* and that I may praise God with thee and with all the Saints forever. I promise thee, O blessed St. Jude, to be ever mindful of this great favor and never cease to honor thee as my special and powerful patron, and to do all in my power gratefully to encourage devotion to thee. Amen.

Prayer to
St. Anthony of Padua

St. Anthony of Padua is invoked in a wide variety of needs but is especially renowned as the "Patron of Lost Objects."

O HOLY ST. ANTHONY, gentlest of Saints, thy love for God and charity for His creatures made thee worthy when on earth to possess miraculous powers. Miracles waited on thy word, which thou wert ever ready to speak for those in trouble or anxiety. Encouraged by this thought, I implore thee to obtain for me . . . *(Here mention your request.)* The answer to my prayer may require a miracle; even so, thou art the Saint of Miracles. O gentle and loving St. Anthony, whose heart was ever full of human sympathy, whisper my petition into the ears of the sweet Infant Jesus, Who loved to be folded in thy arms, and the gratitude of my heart will ever be thine. Amen.

Miraculous Prayer to The Little Flower of Jesus

St. Therese (1873-1897) promised to assist anyone who called upon her for any reason. "I will spend my Heaven in doing good upon earth." "I will let fall a shower of roses."

O LITTLE FLOWER OF JESUS, ever consoling troubled souls with heavenly graces, in thine unfailing intercession I place my confident trust. From the heart of our divine Saviour, petition the blessings of which I stand in greatest need, especially . . . *(here mention your intention)*. Shower upon me thy promised roses of virtue and grace, dear St. Therese, so that swiftly advancing in sanctity and perfect love of neighbor, I may someday receive the crown of life eternal. Amen.

Novena Prayer to St. Philomena
Virgin, Martyr and Wonder-Worker

St. Philomena helps in all sorts of problems, but is particularly invoked for help regarding conversion of sinners, return to the Sacraments, expectant mothers, destitute mothers, problems with children, unhappiness in the home, sterility, priests and their work, help for the sick, the missions, real estate, money problems, food for the poor and mental illness.

O FAITHFUL virgin and glorious martyr, St. Philomena, who works so many miracles on behalf of the poor and sorrowing. Have pity on me; thou knowest the multitude and diversity of my needs. Behold me at thy feet, full of misery, but full of hope. I entreat thy charity, O great Saint! Graciously hear me and obtain from God a favorable answer to the request which I now humbly lay before thee. *(Here mention your petition.)* I am firmly convinced that through thy merits, through the scorn, the sufferings, the death thou didst endure, united to the merits of the Passion and Death of Jesus, thy Spouse, I shall obtain what I ask of thee, and in the joy of my heart I will bless God, Who is admirable in His Saints. Amen.

Prayer to St. Rita
Advocate of the Impossible

O HOLY PATRONESS of those in need, St. Rita, whose pleadings before thy Divine Lord are almost irresistible, who for thy lavishness in granting favors hast been called the Advocate of the Hopeless and even of the Impossible; St. Rita, so humble, so pure, so mortified, so patient and of such compassionate love for thy Crucified Jesus that thou couldst obtain from Him whatsoever thou askest, on account of which all confidently have recourse to thee, expecting, if not always relief, at least comfort; be propitious to our petition, showing thy power with God on behalf of thy suppliant; be lavish to us, as thou hast been in so many wonderful cases, for the greater glory of God, for the spreading of thine own devotion, and for the consolation of those who trust in thee. We promise, if our petition is granted, to glorify thee by making known thy favor, to bless and sing thy praises forever. Relying then upon thy merits and power before the Sacred Heart of Jesus, we pray thee grant that . . . *(Here make your request.)*

Obtain for us our request

By the singular merits of thy childhood,

By thy perfect union with the Divine Will,

By thy heroic sufferings during thy married life,

By the consolation thou didst experience at the conversion of thy husband,

By the sacrifice of thy children rather than see them grievously offend God,

By thy miraculous entrance into the convent,

By thy severe penances and thrice daily bloody scourgings,

By the suffering caused by the wound thou didst receive from the thorn of thy Crucified Saviour,

By the divine love which consumed thy heart,

By that remarkable devotion to the Blessed
Sacrament, on which alone thou didst
exist for four years,
By the happiness with which thou didst part
from thy trials to join thy Divine Spouse,
By the perfect example thou gavest to people of every state of life.

Pray for us, O holy St. Rita, that we may be
made worthy of the promises of Christ.

Let Us Pray

O God, Who in Thine infinite tenderness
hast vouchsafed to regard the prayer of Thy
servant, Blessed Rita, and dost grant to her
supplication that which is impossible to
human foresight, skill and efforts, in reward
of her compassionate love and firm reliance
on Thy promise, have pity on our adversity
and succor us in our calamities, that the
unbeliever may know Thou art the recom-
pense of the humble, the defense of the helpless, and the strength of those who trust in
Thee, through Jesus Christ Our Lord. Amen.

St. Rita, Advocate of the Impossible, pray
for us!

*(St. Rita was an only child of elderly parents; she decided early to
devote her life to God. But her parents made her marry. Her abu-
sive husband was murdered and her two sons, as youths, spoke of
avenging his death. She implored God not to allow them to commit this sin. They both died young, and St. Rita miraculously
entered the Augustinian Order and became one of its greatest
Saints.)*

Prayer to St. Martin de Porres

O GLORIOUS St. Martin de Porres, great Saint of the Dominican Order, look down in mercy upon a poor soul who cries out to thee, and deign to come to my aid in this great need, that I may receive the consolation and succour of Heaven in all my necessities, tribulations and sufferings, but in particular . . . *(here mention your intention).* I thank thee, St. Martin de Porres, for all the help that thou hast given me, both now and in the past, and I promise to be ever grateful to thee and to make thee known to all who are in need of thine assistance. Amen.

Prayer of St. Gertrude The Great

This prayer is reputed to be very powerful in releasing souls from Purgatory.

O ETERNAL Father, I offer Thee the Most Precious Blood of Thy Divine Son Jesus, in union with all the Masses said throughout the world today, for all the holy souls in Purgatory, and for sinners everywhere: for sinners in the Universal Church, for those in my own home and for those within my family. Amen.

(Repeat as many times as desired.)

Prayer to All the Angels
For a Special Favor

BLESS the Lord, all ye His Angels! Thou who art mighty in strength and do His Will, intercede for me at the throne of God. By thine unceasing watchfulness, protect me in every danger of soul and body. Obtain for me the grace of final perseverance, so that after this life, I may be admitted to thy glorious company and sing with thee the praises of God for all eternity.

All ye holy Angels and Archangels, Thrones and Dominations, Principalities and Powers and Virtues of Heaven, Cherubim and Seraphim, and especially thou, my dear Guardian Angel, intercede for me and obtain for me the special favor I now ask. *(Name your intention.)*

Offer the Glory Be *three times.*

Prayers in Honor of the
Seven Sorrows
Of the Blessed Virgin Mary

Approved by Pope Pius VII in 1815. (See the "favors" promised by the Blessed Mother at the end of this prayer.)

V. O God, come to my assistance;
R. *O Lord, make haste to help me.*
V. Glory be to the Father . . .
R. *As it was in the beginning . . .*

1. I grieve for thee, O Mary most sorrowful, in the affliction of thy tender heart at *the prophecy of the holy and aged Simeon.* Dear Mother, by thy heart so afflicted, obtain for me the virtue of humility and the Gift of the holy Fear of God. *Hail Mary . . .*

2. I grieve for thee, O Mary most sorrowful, in the anguish of thy most affectionate heart during *the flight into Egypt* and thy sojourn there. Dear Mother, by thy heart so troubled, obtain for me the virtue of generosity, especially toward the poor, and the Gift of Piety. *Hail Mary . . .*

3. I grieve for thee, O Mary most sorrowful, in those anxieties which tried thy troubled heart at *the loss of thy dear Jesus in the Temple.* Dear Mother, by thy heart so full of anguish, obtain for me the virtue of chastity and the Gift of Knowledge. *Hail Mary . . .*

4. I grieve for thee, O Mary most sorrowful, in the consternation of thy heart at *meeting Jesus as He carried His Cross.* Dear Mother, by thy heart so troubled, obtain for me the virtue of patience and the Gift of Fortitude. *Hail Mary . . .*

5. I grieve for thee, O Mary most sorrowful, in the martyrdom which thy generous heart endured in ***standing near Jesus in His agony on the Cross.*** Dear Mother, by thy afflicted heart, obtain for me the virtue of temperance and the Gift of Counsel. *Hail Mary . . .*

6. I grieve for thee, O Mary most sorrowful, in the wounding of thy compassionate heart, when ***the side of Jesus was struck by the lance before His Body was removed from the Cross.*** Dear Mother, by thy heart thus transfixed, obtain for me the virtue of fraternal charity and the Gift of Understanding. *Hail Mary . . .*

7. I grieve for thee, O Mary most sorrowful, for the pangs that wrenched thy most loving heart at ***the burial of Jesus.*** Dear Mother, by thy heart sunk in the bitterness of desolation, obtain for me the virtue of diligence and the Gift of Wisdom. *Hail Mary . . .*

Let Us Pray

Let intercession be made for us, we beseech Thee, O Lord Jesus Christ, now and at the hour of our death, before the throne of Thy mercy, by the Blessed Virgin Mary, Thy Mother, whose most holy soul was pierced by a sword of sorrow in the hour of Thy bitter Passion, through Thee, O Jesus Christ, Saviour of the world, Who with the

Father and the Holy Ghost lives and reigns
world without end. Amen.

According to St. Bridget of Sweden (1303-1373), the
Blessed Virgin grants the following favors to those who
honor her daily by saying seven *Hail Marys*, while meditating on her tears and sorrows: 1. "I will grant peace to
their families."   2. "They will be enlightened about the
divine Mysteries."   3. "I will console them in their pains,
and I will accompany them in their work."   4. "I will give
them as much as they ask for, as long so it does not oppose
the adorable Will of my divine Son or the sanctification
of their souls."   5. "I will defend them in their spiritual
battles with the infernal enemy, and I will protect them
at every instant of their lives."   6. "I will visibly help them
at the moment of their death—they will see the face of
their mother."   7. "I have obtained this grace from my
divine Son, that those who propagate this devotion to my
tears and dolors will be taken directly from this earthly
life to eternal happiness, since all their sins will be for-
given and my Son will be their eternal consolation and
joy."

Prayer to St. Expeditus
"Patron of Youth," "Advocate in Urgent Cases" and "Mediator in Lawsuits"
For a Quick Solution to a Problem, Or to Cure Procrastination

St. Expeditus (4th Century) was a young Roman soldier, believed
to have been martyred for his Faith at Militene, Armenia. He is
very powerful to bring speedy help in urgent cases.

O ST. EXPEDITUS, we humbly beg thee
to come to our aid so that thy prompt
and certain intercession will obtain for us,

from our Divine Lord, the grace of a happy and swift solution to the matter which now concerns us. *(Mention your intention.)* We do so without fear, being fully confident in the supreme wisdom of Our Blessed Lord, and place our trust in Him without reservation, being mindful that His will alone be done. Amen.

Holy Mary, Mother of God, *Pray for us.*

St. Expeditus, our help in urgent matters, *Pray for us.*

(Repeat the above prayer one time and then offer three times the Our Father, Hail Mary, and Glory Be.)

Short Novena Litany to St. Expeditus

O ST. EXPEDITUS, who didst receive from the Lord the crown of righteousness which He has promised to those who love Him, *pray for us.*
Patron of Youth, *pray for us.*
Help of Scholars, *etc.*
Model of Soldiers,
Protector of Travelers,
Advocate of Sinners,
Health of the Sick,

Consolation of the Afflicted,
Mediator of Lawsuits,
Our help in urgent matters,
Who dost teach us never to defer,
Ardent and trusting in prayer,
Most faithful support of those who hope in
    thee,
Whose protection at the hour of death
    insures salvation.

Lamb of God, Who takest away the sins of
    the world, *Spare us, O Lord.*
Lamb of God, Who takest away the sins of
    the world, *Graciously hear us, O Lord.*
Lamb of God, Who takest away the sins of
    the world, *Have Mercy on us, O Lord.*

V. Pray for us, St. Expeditus,
R. *That we may be made worthy of the
    promises of Christ.*

Let Us Pray

Almighty and Eternal God, Who art the
consolation of the afflicted and the support
of those in pain, deign to receive the cries of
our distress, so that by the intercession and
merits of Thy glorious martyr, St. Expeditus, we may joyfully experience in our
extreme necessity the help of Thy mercy,
through Christ Our Lord. Amen.

(Repeat the above litany one time and then offer one Our Father, Hail Mary and Glory Be in thanksgiving for any favors received.)

A Most Efficacious Prayer To Our Lady of Mt. Carmel
(Never Found to Fail)

O MOST BEAUTIFUL FLOWER of Mount Carmel, Fruitful Vine, Splendor of Heaven, Blessed Mother of the Son of God, Immaculate Virgin, assist me in this my necessity. *(Mention your intention.)* O Star of the Sea, help me and show me in this that thou art my Mother.

O Holy Mary, Mother of God, Queen of Heaven and Earth, I humbly beseech thee, from the bottom of my heart, to succour me in this necessity; there are none that can withstand thy power. O, show me in this that thou art my Mother.

O Mary, conceived without sin, pray for us who have recourse to thee. *(3 times).*

Sweet Mother, I place this cause in thy hands. *(3 times).*

It is suggested to offer three times the *Our Father, Hail Mary,* and *Glory Be* in thanksgiving.

A Daily Consecration
To the Holy Spirit

O MOST Holy Spirit, receive the consecration that I make of my entire being. From this moment on, come into every area of my life and into each of my actions. Thou art my Light, my Guide, my Strength and the sole desire of my heart. I abandon myself without reserve to Thy divine action, and I desire to be ever docile to Thine inspirations. O Holy Spirit, transform me with and through Mary into "another Christ Jesus," for the glory of the Father and the salvation of the world. Amen.

Dedication Prayer
Of St. Colette

O BLESSED JESUS, I dedicate myself to Thee in health, in illness, in my life and in my death, in all my desires, in all my deeds, so that I may never work henceforth except for Thy glory, for the salvation of souls, and for that which Thou hast chosen me. From this moment on, Dearest Lord, there is nothing which I am not prepared to undertake for love of Thee.

—Saint Colette of Jesus (1381-1447)
Reformer of the Poor Clares

A Morning Offering

O MY JESUS, here is my tongue, that Thou mayest watch over it, that it may not utter more than pleases Thee, and that my silence may speak to Thee. Here are my ears, that they may listen only to the voice of duty and to Thy Voice, O Jesus! Here are my eyes, that they may not cease to behold Thee in every face and in every work. Here are my hands and my feet, that Thou mayest make them agile, that they may be riveted to Thy service alone and to the execution of Thy desires. Here are my thoughts, that Thy Light may possess them. Here is my heart, that Thy Love, O Jesus, may reign and rest in it!

—Sister Mary of the Holy Trinity
Poor Clare of Jerusalem

A Prayer of
St. Ignatius Loyola (1491-1556)

DEAREST LORD, teach me to be generous. Teach me to serve Thee as Thou deservest: to give and not to count the cost; to fight and not to heed the wounds; to toil and not to seek for rest; to labor and not to seek reward, save that of knowing that I do Thy Will, O God.

An Act of Oblation

O ETERNAL FATHER, we offer Thee the Blood, the Passion and the Death of Jesus Christ, the sorrows of Mary most holy and of Saint Joseph, in satisfaction for our sins, for the aid of the Holy Souls in Purgatory, for the needs of Holy Mother Church and for the conversion of sinners. Amen.

Prayer to Mary
Mistress of the Angels

Given by Mary to a Bernardine Sister approximately 1937 and urged fervently by Our Lady to be printed and distributed.

O EXALTED QUEEN of Heaven, Supreme Mistress of the Angels, who from the beginning has received from God the power and the commission to crush the serpent's head, we pray thee humbly, send down thy Holy Legions, that they, under thy command and power, may pursue the spirits of Hell, everywhere wage war against them, defeat their boldness and thrust them into the abyss of Hell.

"Who is like unto God?" "Holy Angels and Archangels, defend us and protect us!" "O kind and tender Mother, thou shalt ever remain our love and our hope." Amen.

Indulgenced Prayer to Mary "Mother of Good Counsel"

O MOST GLORIOUS VIRGIN, chosen from among all others by an eternal decree to be the Mother of the Eternal Word, the Treasury of Divine Graces and the Refuge of Sinners, I, thy most unworthy servant, have recourse to thee, that thou mayest be my tender guide and counsellor in this valley of tears. Through the Precious Blood of thy Son, obtain for me the pardon of my sins, the salvation of my soul, and all things necessary to attain them. Grant also that Holy Church may triumph over her enemies and that the Kingdom of Jesus Christ will soon be extended over the whole earth. I ask all this through thy intercession. Amen.

Blessed Be the Hour

This prayer is reputed to have been composed by St. Colette (1381-1447), Reformer of the Poor Clares. It is piously believed that whoever recites this prayer fifteen times a day from the Feast of St. Andrew (November 30) until Christmas will obtain what is asked.

BLESSED be the hour and the moment in which the Son of God was born of the most pure Virgin Mary, at midnight, in Bethlehem, in piercing cold. In that hour vouchsafe, O my God, to hear my prayer and grant my desires, through the merits of Our Saviour Jesus Christ, and of His blessed Mother. Amen.

A Short Consecration to the Blessed Virgin Mary
By St. Alphonsus Liguori

O HOLY MARY, my Mistress, into thy blessed trust and special keeping, into the bosom of thy tender mercy, I commend my soul and my body this day, every day of my life and at the hour of my death. To thee I entrust all my hopes and consolations, all my trials and miseries, my life and the end of my life, that through thy most holy intercession and thy merits, all my actions may be ordered and disposed according to thy will and that of thy Divine Son. Amen.

Chaplet of the Divine Mercy

Using the Rosary beads, begin by reciting: one
Our Father, *one* Hail Mary *and one* Apostle's Creed.
*On the Our Father beads say this prayer, which was
given by Our Lord to St. Faustina (1905-1938):*

ETERNAL Father, I offer Thee the Body
and Blood, Soul and Divinity of Thy
dearly beloved Son, Our Lord Jesus Christ,
in atonement for our sins and those of the
whole world.

On the Hail Mary beads say:

FOR the sake of His sorrowful Passion,
have mercy on us and on the whole
world.

In conclusion, say three times:

HOLY God, Holy Mighty One, Holy
Immortal One, have mercy on us and
on the whole world.

Aspirations for any Occasion

We adore Thee, O Christ, and we praise
Thee, because of Thy Holy Cross, Thou hast
redeemed the world!

Blessed be Jesus in the Most Holy Sacrament of the Altar.

Salutations to Mary

These Salutations to Mary were written by St. John Eudes (1601-1680) and promoted in this version by the Servant of God, Father Paul of Moll (1824-1896). The venerable Father Paul assured one of his friends that those who devoutly venerate Mary with these salutations may rely on her powerful protection and blessing. He said further that it is impossible not to be heard favorably when we recite these Salutations to Mary for the conversion of sinners.

Hail Mary, Daughter of God the Father!

Hail Mary, Mother of God the Son!

Hail Mary, Spouse of God the Holy Ghost!

Hail Mary, Temple of the Most Blessed Trinity!

Hail Mary, Pure Lily of the Effulgent Trinity!

Hail Mary, Celestial Rose of the ineffable Love of God!

Hail Mary, Virgin pure and humble, of whom the King of Heaven willed to be born and with thy milk to be nourished!

Hail Mary, Virgin of Virgins!

Hail Mary, Queen of Martyrs, whose soul a sword transfixed!

Hail Mary, Lady most blessed unto whom all power in Heaven and earth is given!

Hail Mary, My Queen and my Mother, my Life, my sweetness and my Hope!

Hail Mary, Mother most Amiable!

Hail Mary, Mother most Admirable!

Hail Mary, Mother of Divine Love!

Hail Mary, IMMACULATE, Conceived without sin!

Hail Mary, Full of Grace, The Lord is with Thee! Blessed art Thou among Women, and Blessed be the Fruit of thy womb, JESUS.

Blessed be thy Spouse, St. Joseph.
Blessed be thy Father, St. Joachim.
Blessed be thy Mother, St. Anne.
Blessed be thy Guardian, St. John.
Blessed be thy Holy Angel, St. Gabriel.

Glory be to God the Father, Who chose thee!
Glory be to God the Son, Who loved thee!
Glory be to God the Holy Ghost, Who espoused thee!
O Glorious Virgin Mary, may all men love and praise thee!
Holy Mary, Mother of God, pray for us and bless us, now and at death, in the Name of JESUS, thy Divine Son! Amen.

Novena of Confidence
To the Sacred Heart

O LORD Jesus Christ, to Thy most Sacred Heart I confide this intention *(Name your request)*. Only look upon me, then do what Thy love inspires. Let Thy Sacred Heart decide. I count on Thee. I trust in Thee. I throw myself on Thy mercy. O Lord Jesus, Thou wilt not fail me.

Sacred Heart of Jesus, I trust in Thee!

Sacred Heart of Jesus, I believe in Thy love for me!

Sacred Heart of Jesus, Thy kingdom come!

Sacred Heart of Jesus, I have asked Thee for many favors, but I earnestly implore this one. Take it and place it in Thine open Heart. When the Eternal Father looks upon it, He will see it covered with Thy Precious Blood. It will be no longer my prayer, but Thine, O Jesus.

Heart of Jesus, I place all my trust in Thee! Let me not be disappointed. Amen.

Offering of St. Ignatius Loyola
"Suscipe"

TAKE, O Lord, and receive my entire liberty, my memory, my understanding and my whole will. All that I am and all that I possess Thou hast given me: I surrender it all to Thee to be disposed of according to Thy will. Give me only Thy love and Thy grace; with these I will be rich enough and will desire nothing more.

(Those who like this prayer should read The Gift of Oneself *by Fr. Joseph Schryvers, C.SS.R.)*

Memorare to Our Lady of The Sacred Heart

REMEMBER, Our Lady of the Sacred Heart, the ineffable power which thy Divine Son has given thee over His adorable Heart. Full of confidence in thy merits, we now implore thy protection. O Heavenly Treasurer of the Heart of Jesus, of that Heart which is the inexhaustible source of all graces and which thou dost open when it pleases thee, in order to distribute among men all the treasures of love and mercy, of light and salvation which it contains: grant us, we beseech thee, the favors we request. *(Mention your requests.)* No, we cannot meet with a refusal, and since thou art our Mother, Our Lady of the Sacred Heart, favorably hear and grant our prayers. Amen.

Prayer to One's Patron Saint

GREAT ST. *(Name)*, who at my Baptism was chosen as my guardian and under whose patronage I became an adopted child of God and solemnly renounced Satan, his works and allurements, assist me by thy powerful intercession in the fulfillment of these sacred promises. Help me to love God above all things and always to live in the state of grace. Finally, obtain for me the grace of a happy death, so that thou mayest welcome me into Heaven for all eternity. Amen.

Prayer of St. Francis of Assisi

LORD, make me an instrument
   of Thy peace.
Where there is hatred, let me
   sow love;
where there is injury, pardon;
   where there is doubt, faith;
where there is despair, hope;
   where there is darkness, light;
   and where there is sadness, joy.
O Divine Master, grant that
   I may not so much seek to be
consoled as to console; to be
   understood as to understand;
to be loved as to love;
   for it is in giving that we receive;
it is in pardoning that we are
   pardoned;
and it is in dying that we are
   born to eternal life.

Prayer to Christ The King

O CHRIST JESUS, I acknowledge Thee King of the universe. All that has been created has been made for Thee. Exercise over me all Thy sovereign rights.

I renew the promises of my Baptism. I renounce Satan and all his works, and all his pomps, and I promise to live a good Christian life and to do all in my power to procure the triumph of the rights of God and Thy Church.

Divine Heart of Jesus, I offer Thee my poor efforts in order to obtain that all hearts may acknowledge Thy Sacred Royalty, and that thus the Kingdom of Thy peace may be established throughout the universe. Amen.

Aspirations for any Occasion

We adore Thee, O Christ, and we praise Thee, because by Thy holy Cross Thou hast redeemed the world.

May the Heart of Jesus in the Most Blessed Sacrament be praised, adored and loved with grateful affection, at every moment, in all the tabernacles of the world, even to the End of Time! Amen.

An Act of Consecration of the Human Race to The Sacred Heart of Jesus

According to former rules governing indulgences, a plenary indulgence could be gained once a month by pious recitation of this prayer and by fulfilling the other requirements for gaining a plenary indulgence.

O MOST sweet Jesus, Redeemer of the human race, look down upon us humbly prostrate before Thine altar. We are Thine, and Thine we wish to be; but to be more surely united with Thee, behold, each one of us freely consecrates himself today to Thy most Sacred Heart. Many indeed have never known Thee; many, too, despising Thy precepts, have rejected Thee. Have mercy on them all, most merciful Jesus, and draw them to Thy Sacred Heart. Be Thou King, O Lord, not only of the faithful who have never forsaken Thee, but also of the prodigal children who have abandoned Thee; grant that they may quickly return to their Father's house, lest they die of wretchedness and hunger. Be Thou King of those who are deceived by erroneous opinions, or whom discord keeps aloof, and call them back to the harbor of truth and unity of faith, so that soon there may be but one flock and one Shepherd. Grant, O Lord, to Thy Church assurance of freedom and immunity from harm; give peace and order to all nations, and make the earth resound from pole to pole with one cry: "Praise be to the Divine Heart that wrought our salvation; to It be glory and honor forever." Amen.

An Act of Reparation to the Sacred Heart of Jesus

According to former rules governing indulgences, a plenary indulgence could be gained once a month by pious recitation of this prayer and by fulfilling the other requirements for gaining a plenary indulgence.

O SWEET JESUS, Whose overflowing charity for men is requited by so much forgetfulness, negligence and contempt, behold us prostrate before Thy altar, eager to repair by a special act of homage the cruel indifference and injuries to which Thy loving Heart is everywhere subject.

Mindful, alas, that we ourselves have had a share in such great indignities, which we now deplore from the bottom of our hearts, we humbly ask Thy pardon and declare our readiness to atone by voluntary expiation, not only for our own personal offenses, but also for the sins of those who, straying far from the path of salvation, refuse in their obstinate infidelity to follow Thee, their Shepherd and Leader, or renouncing the vows of their Baptism, have cast off the sweet yoke of Thy law. We are now resolved

to expiate each and every deplorable out-
rage committed against Thee; we are deter-
mined to make amends for the manifold
offenses against Christian modesty in unbe-
coming dress and behavior, for all the foul
seductions laid to ensnare the feet of the
innocent, for the frequent violation of Sundays and Holy Days and for the shocking
blasphemies uttered against Thee and Thy
Saints. We wish also to make amends for the
insults to which Thy Vicar on earth and Thy
priests are subjected, for the profanation, by
conscious neglect or terrible acts of sacrilege
of the very Sacrament of Thy divine love;
and lastly for the public crimes of nations
which resist the rights and the teaching
authority of the Church which Thou hast
founded.

Would, O divine Jesus, we were able to
wash away such abominations with our
blood. We now offer in reparation for these
violations of Thy divine honor, the satisfaction Thou didst once make to Thy eternal
Father on the Cross and which Thou dost
continue to renew daily on our altars; we
offer it in union with the acts of atonement
of Thy Virgin Mother and all the Saints and
of the pious faithful on earth; and we sincerely promise to make reparation, as far as
we can, with the help of Thy grace, for all

neglect of Thy great love and for the sins we and others have committed in the past. Henceforth we will live a life of unwavering faith, of purity of conduct, of perfect observance of the precepts of the Gospel, and especially that of charity. We promise, to the best of our power, to prevent others from offending Thee and to bring as many as possible to follow Thee.

O loving Jesus, through the intercession of the Blessed Virgin Mary, our model in reparation, deign to receive the voluntary offering we make of this act of expiation; and by the crowning gift of perseverance, keep us faithful unto death in our duty and allegiance we owe to Thee, so that we may all one day come to that happy home, where Thou, with the Father and the Holy Spirit, livest and reignest, God, world without end. Amen.

Aspirations for any Occasion

O Sacrament Most Holy, O Sacrament Divine, all praise and all thanksgiving be every moment Thine!

Jesus, Mary and Joseph, I love Thee; please save souls!

The Magnificat
(*Words of Our Lady from* Luke 1:46-55.)

MY SOUL doth magnify the Lord, and my spirit hath rejoiced in God my Saviour, because He hath regarded the humility of His handmaid: for behold, from henceforth all generations shall call me blessed, because He that is mighty hath done great things to me, and holy is His Name. And His mercy is from generation unto generations, to them that fear Him.

He hath showed might in His arm: He hath scattered the proud in the conceit of their heart. He hath put down the mighty from their seat, and hath exalted the humble. He hath filled the hungry with good things, and the rich He hath sent away empty. He hath received Israel His servant, being mindful of His mercy: as He spoke to our fathers, to Abraham and to his seed forever.

Aspirations for any Occasion

Immaculate Heart of Mary, pray for us now and at the hour of our death. Amen.

O Queen of the Angels, pray for us!

The Litany of The Blessed Virgin Mary

(The Litany of Loreto)

(For public or private use.)

Lord, have mercy on us.
   Christ, have mercy on us.
Lord, have mercy on us. Christ, hear us.
   Christ, graciously hear us.
God the Father of Heaven,
   Have mercy on us.
God the Son, Redeemer of the world,
   Have mercy on us.
God the Holy Ghost,
   Have mercy on us.
Holy Trinity, One God,
   Have mercy on us.

Holy Mary, *pray for us.*
Holy Mother of God, *pray for us.*
Holy Virgin of virgins, *etc.*
Mother of Christ,
Mother of divine grace,
Mother most pure,
Mother most chaste,
Mother inviolate,
Mother undefiled,
Mother most amiable,
Mother most admirable,
Mother of good counsel,
Mother of our Creator,

Mother of our Saviour,
Virgin most prudent,
Virgin most venerable,
Virgin most renowned,
Virgin most powerful,
Virgin most merciful,
Virgin most faithful,
Mirror of Justice,
Seat of Wisdom,
Cause of our Joy,
Spiritual Vessel,
Vessel of Honor,
Singular Vessel of Devotion,
Mystical Rose,
Tower of David,
Tower of Ivory,
House of Gold,
Ark of the Covenant,
Gate of Heaven,
Morning Star,
Health of the Sick,
Refuge of Sinners,
Comforter of the Afflicted,
Help of Christians,
Queen of Angels,
Queen of Patriarchs,
Queen of Prophets,
Queen of Apostles,
Queen of Martyrs,
Queen of Confessors,

Queen of Virgins,
Queen of all Saints,
Queen Conceived without Original Sin,
Queen Assumed into Heaven,
Queen of the Most Holy Rosary,
Queen of Peace,

Lamb of God, Who takest away the sins of
the world,
Spare us, O Lord.
Lamb of God, Who takest away the sins of
the world,
Graciously hear us, O Lord.
Lamb of God, Who takest away the sins of
the world,
Have mercy on us.

V. Pray for us, O holy Mother of God,
R. *That we may be made worthy of the
promises of Christ.*

Let Us Pray

Grant, we beseech Thee, O Lord God, that
we Thy servants may enjoy perpetual health
of mind and body, and by the glorious intercession of the Blessed Mary, ever Virgin, be
delivered from present sorrow and enjoy
everlasting happiness. Through Christ Our
Lord. Amen.

Prayer to St. Joseph

Prescribed by Pope Leo XIII, for the month of October, after the recitation of the Rosary and the Litany of Our Lady, but it can be said fruitfully at any time after praying to Mary.

UNTO THEE, O blessed Joseph, do we fly in our tribulation, and having implored the help of thy holy Spouse, we now also confidently seek thy protection. By that affection which united thee to the Immaculate Virgin, Mother of God, and by thy fatherly love for the Child Jesus, we humbly beg thee to look down with compassion upon the inheritance which Jesus Christ has purchased with His blood and in our need to help us by thy powerful intercession.

Do thou, O prudent Guardian of the Holy Family, watch over the chosen people of Jesus Christ. Keep us, O loving father, safe from all error and corruption. O great protector, from thy place in Heaven, graciously help us in our contest against the powers of darkness. And as of old thou didst rescue the Child Jesus from the danger of death, so now defend God's Holy Church from the snares of the enemy and from all adversity. Extend to each one of us thy continual protection, that led on by thine example and strengthened by thine aid, we may live and die in holiness and obtain everlasting happiness in Heaven. Amen.

Litany of St. Joseph
(For public or private use.)

Lord, have mercy on us.
  Christ, have mercy on us.
Lord, have mercy on us. Christ, hear us.
  Christ, graciously hear us.
God the Father of Heaven,
  Have mercy on us.
God the Son, Redeemer of the world,
  Have mercy on us.
God the Holy Ghost,
  Have mercy on us.
Holy Trinity, One God,
  Have mercy on us.

Holy Mary, *pray for us.*
St. Joseph, *pray for us.*
Renowned Offspring of David, *etc.*
Light of Patriarchs,
Spouse of the Mother of God,
Chaste Guardian of the Virgin,
Foster Father of the Son of God,
Diligent Protector of Christ,
Head of the Holy Family,
Joseph most just,
Joseph most chaste,
Joseph most prudent,
Joseph most strong,
Joseph most obedient,

Joseph most faithful,
Mirror of Patience,
Lover of Poverty,
Model of Artisans,
Glory of domestic life,
Guardian of Virgins,
Pillar of Families,
Solace of the Afflicted,
Hope of the Sick,
Patron of the Dying,
Terror of Demons,
Protector of Holy Church,

Lamb of God, Who takest away
　the sins of the world,
　　Spare us, O Lord!
Lamb of God, Who takest away
　the sins of the world,
　　Graciously hear us, O Lord!
Lamb of God, Who takest away
　the sins of the world,
　　Have mercy on us.

V. He made him the lord of His household.
R. *And prince over all His possessions.*

Let Us Pray

O GOD, Who in Thine ineffable Providence didst vouchsafe to choose Blessed Joseph to be the spouse of Thy most holy Mother, grant, we beseech Thee, that we may have for our advocate in Heaven him whom we venerate as our protector on earth, Who livest and reignest world without end. Amen.

The *Te Deum*
(A Hymn of Thanksgiving)

1. We praise Thee, O God; we acknowledge Thee to be the Lord.
2. Thee, the Father everlasting, all the earth doth worship.
3. To Thee all the Angels, to Thee the heavens, and all the Powers,
4. To Thee the Cherubim and Seraphim cry out without ceasing:
5. "Holy, holy, holy, Lord God of hosts."
6. Full are the heavens and the earth of the majesty of Thy glory.
7. Thee, the glorious choir of the Apostles,
8. Thee, the admirable company of the Prophets,
9. Thee, the white-robed army of martyrs doth praise.
10. Thee, the Holy Church throughout the world doth confess:
11. The Father, of incomprehensible majesty,
12. Thine adorable, true, and only Son,
13. And the Holy Spirit, the Paraclete.

14. Thou, O Christ, art the King of glory.
15. Thou art the everlasting Son of the Father.
16. Thou, having taken upon Thee to deliver man, didst not disdain the Virgin's womb.
17. Thou, having overcome the sting of death, hast opened to believers the Kingdom of Heaven.
18. Thou sittest at the right hand of God, in the glory of the Father.
19. Thou, we believe, art the Judge to come.
20. We beseech Thee, therefore, to help Thy servants, whom Thou hast redeemed with Thy Precious Blood.
21. Make them to be numbered with Thy Saints in glory everlasting.
22. O Lord, save Thy people and bless Thine inheritance,
23. And govern them and exalt them forever.
24. Day by day we bless Thee,
25. And we praise Thy name forever; yea, forever and ever.
26. Vouchsafe, O Lord, this day to keep us without sin.
27. Have mercy on us, O Lord; have mercy on us.
28. Let Thy mercy, O Lord, be upon us, as we have trusted in Thee.

29. In Thee, O Lord, have I trusted: let me not be confounded forever.

V. Let us bless the Father and the Son with the Holy Spirit.
R. *Let us praise and exalt Him forever.*
V. Blessed art Thou, O Lord, in the firmament of Heaven.
R. *And worthy of praise, and glorious, and exalted above all forever.*
V. O Lord, hear my prayer.
R. *And let my cry come to Thee.*
V. The Lord be with thee.
R. *And with thy spirit.*

Let Us Pray

O God, of Thy mercies there is no number, and of Thy goodness the treasure is infinite; we render thanks to Thy most gracious Majesty for the gifts Thou hast bestowed upon us, evermore imploring Thy clemency, that as Thou dost grant the petitions of them that ask Thee, Thou mayest never forsake them, but may prepare them for the rewards to come. Through Christ Our Lord. Amen.

Morning Prayers

An Act of Faith in
The Presence of God

O MY GOD, I firmly believe that Thou art here present and dost plainly see me, that Thou dost observe all my actions, all my thoughts, and the most secret movements of my heart. I acknowledge that I am not worthy to come into Thy presence, nor to lift up my eyes to Thee, because I have so often sinned against Thee. But Thy goodness and mercy invite me to come to Thee; help me, I implore Thee, with Thy holy grace, and teach me to pray to Thee as I ought.

An Act of Adoration
And Thanksgiving

O ETERNAL God, Father, Son and Holy Spirit, the beginning and end of all things, in Whom we live and move and have our being, prostrate before Thee in body and soul, I adore Thee with the most profound humility. I bless Thee and give Thee thanks for all the benefits Thou hast conferred upon me, especially that Thou hast created me out of nothing, made me after Thine own image and likeness, redeemed me with the

Precious Blood of Thy Son, and sanctified me with Thy Holy Spirit. I thank Thee that Thou hast called me into Thy Church, helped me by Thy grace, admitted me to Thy Sacraments, watched over me by Thy special Providence, blessed me, notwithstanding my sins and unworthiness, with Thy continuing and gracious protection, and for all the innumerable blessings which I owe to Thine undeserved bounty. I thank Thee especially for having preserved me during the past night and for bringing me in safety to the beginning of another day. What return can I make to Thee, my God, for all that Thou hast done for me? I will bless Thy Holy Name and serve Thee all the days of my life. Bless the Lord, my soul, and let all that is within me praise His Holy Name.

An Act of Faith

O MY GOD, I firmly believe in all that Thy Holy, Catholic and Apostolic Church approves and teaches, since it is Thou, the Infallible Truth, Who hast revealed it to Thy Church.

An Act of Hope

O MY GOD, with a firm confidence I hope in Thee, that Thou wilt grant me, through the merits of Jesus Christ, the assistance of Thy grace, and that after my keeping Thy commandments, Thou wilt bestow on me life everlasting, according to Thy promises, Thou Who art almighty and Whose word is truth!

An Act of Charity

O MY GOD, I love Thee with my whole heart, with my whole soul, with all my strength, and above all things, because Thou art infinitely good and infinitely lovable. Also, for love of Thee do I love my neighbor as myself.

An Act of Contrition, With Good Resolutions

Here call to mind the chief sins of your past life and make resolutions against the temptations and dangerous occasions you may meet with this day.

O MY GOD, how little have I served Thee in time past! How greatly have I sinned against Thee! I acknowledge my iniquity, and my sin is always before me. But I repent, O Lord, I repent. I am heartily sorry that I have spent that time in offending Thee which Thou hast given to me to be employed in Thy service, in advancing the good of my own soul and obtaining everlasting life. I am sorry above all things that I have offended Thee, because Thou art infinitely good and sin is infinitely displeasing to Thee. I desire to love Thee with my whole heart, and I firmly purpose, by the help of Thy grace, to serve Thee more faithfully in the time to come.

Accept, I implore Thee, the offering I now make to Thee of the remainder of my life. I renew the vows and promises made in my Baptism. I renounce the devil and all his works, the world and all its pomps. I now begin and will endeavor to spend this day according to Thy holy Will, performing all my actions in a manner pleasing to Thee. I will take particular care to avoid the failings I am so apt to commit and to exercise the virtues most agreeable to my state and employment.

To Our Guardian Angel

O ANGEL of God, who art appointed by divine mercy to be my guardian, enlighten and protect, direct and govern me this day. Amen.

Evening Prayers

The official evening prayer of the Church, and the best of all, is Compline. Here follows, however, an alternative form of evening prayers. (Note: The cross signifies that one is supposed to make the Sign of the Cross at this point in the prayer.)

In the name of the ✠ Father, and of the Son, and of the Holy Ghost. Amen.

Blessed be the holy and undivided Trinity, now and for ever. Amen.

Our Father, Hail Mary, Glory Be, Apostles' Creed.

V. Come, Holy Ghost, fill the hearts of Thy faithful,

R. *And kindle in them the fire of Thy love.*

V. Send forth Thy Spirit, and they shall be created,

R. *And Thou shalt renew the face of the earth.*

Let Us Pray

O God, Who hast instructed the hearts of the Faithful by the light of the Holy Ghost, grant us, we beseech Thee, that by the gift of the same Spirit we may always be truly wise and ever rejoice in His consolation, through Jesus Christ Our Lord. Amen.

Place yourself in the presence of God and give Him thanks for all the benefits which you have received from Him, particularly this day.

O MY GOD, I firmly believe that Thou art here present and dost plainly see me, and that Thou dost observe all my actions, all my thoughts and the most secret motions of my heart. Thou dost watch over me with an incomparable love, every moment bestowing favors and preserving me from evil. Blessed be Thy Holy Name, and may all creatures bless Thy goodness for the benefits which I have ever received from Thee, and particularly this day. May the Saints and Angels supply my defect in rendering Thee due thanks. Never permit me to be so base and wicked as to repay Thy goodness with ingratitude and Thy blessings with offenses and injuries.

You should here ask of Our Lord Jesus Christ for the grace to discover the sins which you have committed this day and beg of Him a true sorrow for them and sincere repentance.

O MY LORD JESUS CHRIST, Judge of the living and the dead, before Whom I must appear one day to give an exact account of my whole life, enlighten me, I implore Thee, and give me a humble and contrite heart, that I may see wherein I have offended Thine infinite Majesty, and judge myself now with such a just severity, that then Thou mayest judge me with mercy and clemency.

You should endeavor, as far as possible, to put yourself in the disposition in which you desire to be found at the hour of death.

O MY GOD, I accept death as a homage and an adoration which I owe to Thy divine Majesty and as a punishment justly due to my sins, in union with the death of my Dear Redeemer and as the only means of coming to Thee, my beginning and Last End.

I firmly believe all the sacred truths which the Holy Catholic and Apostolic Church believes and teaches, because Thou hast revealed them. And by the assistance of Thy holy grace, I am resolved to live and to die in communion with this, Thy Church.

Relying upon Thy goodness, power and promises, I hope to obtain pardon of my sins and life everlasting, through the merits of Thy Son Jesus Christ, my only Redeemer, and by the intercession of His Blessed Mother and all the Saints.

I love Thee with all my heart and soul, and I desire to love Thee as the blessed do in Heaven. I adore all the designs of Thy Divine Providence, resigning myself entirely to Thy holy Will. I also love my neighbor for Thy sake, as I love myself.

I sincerely forgive all who have injured me, and ask pardon of all whom I have injured.

I renounce the devil, and all his works; the world, and all its pomps; the flesh, and all its temptations.

I desire to be dissolved and to be with Christ.

Father, into Thy hands I commend my spirit.

Jesus, Mary, and Joseph, I give thee my heart and my soul.

Jesus, Mary, and Joseph, assist me in my last agony.

Jesus, Mary, and Joseph, may I breathe forth my soul in peace with thee. Amen.

Lord Jesus, receive my soul.

May the Blessed Virgin Mary, St. Joseph and all the Saints pray for us to Our Lord, that we may be preserved this night from sin and all evils. Amen.

O Blessed St. Michael, defend us in the day of battle, that we may not be lost at the dreadful Judgment. Amen.

O Angel of God, who art appointed by divine mercy to be my guardian, enlighten and protect, direct and govern me this night. Amen.

May Almighty God have mercy on us, forgive us our sins and bring us to life everlasting. Amen.

May the Almighty and Merciful Lord grant us ✛ pardon, absolution and remission of all our sins. Amen.

— *End of Evening Prayers* —

Anima Christi

Soul of Christ, sanctify me;
  Body of Christ, save me;
Blood of Christ, inebriate me;
  Water from the side of Christ, wash me.

Passion of Christ, strengthen me;
  O good Jesus, hear me;
Within Thy wounds hide me;
  Suffer me not to be separated from Thee.

From the malignant enemy defend me;
  In the hour of my death, call me,
And bid me come to Thee,
  That, with Thy Saints, I may praise Thee
Forever and ever. Amen.

Aspirations for any Occasion

Most Sacred Heart of Jesus, have mercy on us!

My Jesus, I trust in Thee!

The Divine Praises

Traditionally recited publicly at the end of Benediction of the Blessed Sacrament, just before the Host is returned to the tabernacle. It may be recited privately at any time as an act of praise and thanksgiving.

BLESSED be God.
Blessed be His Holy Name.
Blessed be Jesus Christ, true God and true man.
Blessed be the Name of Jesus.
Blessed be His Most Sacred Heart.
Blessed be His Most Precious Blood.
Blessed be Jesus in the Most Holy Sacrament of the Altar.
Blessed be the Holy Ghost, the Paraclete.
Blessed be the great Mother of God, Mary most holy.
Blessed be her holy and Immaculate Conception.
Blessed be her glorious Assumption.
Blessed be the name of Mary, Virgin and Mother.
Blessed be St. Joseph, her most chaste spouse.
Blessed be God, in His Angels and in His Saints.

Prayer Before a Crucifix

BEHOLD, O kind and most sweet Jesus, before Thy face I humbly kneel, and with the most fervent desire of my soul, I pray and beseech Thee to impress upon my heart lively sentiments of faith, hope and charity, true contrition for my sins and a firm purpose of amendment, while with deep affection and grief of soul, I ponder within myself, mentally contemplating Thy five most precious wounds, having before my eyes the words which David the Prophet spoke concerning Thee: "They have pierced my hands and my feet; they have numbered all my bones." (*Psalm* 21:17-18).

The Five Fatima Prayers

The Pardon Prayer

MY GOD, I believe, I adore, I hope and I love Thee! I ask pardon of Thee for those who do not believe, do not adore, do not hope and do not love Thee.

The Angel's Prayer

MOST Holy Trinity, Father, Son and Holy Ghost, I adore Thee profoundly. I offer Thee the Most Precious Body, Blood, Soul and Divinity of Jesus Christ, present in all the tabernacles of the world, in reparation for the outrages, sacrileges and indifferences by which He Himself is offended. And through the infinite merits of His Most Sacred Heart, and the Immaculate Heart of Mary, I beg of Thee the conversion of poor sinners.

Blessed Sacrament Prayer

O MOST Holy Trinity, I adore Thee! My God, my God, I love Thee in the Most Blessed Sacrament!

Sacrifice Prayer

Our Lady of Fatima said: Sacrifice yourselves for sinners, and say many times, especially whenever you make some sacrifice:

O JESUS, I offer this for love of Thee, for the conversion of sinners, and in reparation for the sins committed against the Immaculate Heart of Mary.

O My Jesus

To be said after the Glory Be *following each decade of the Rosary.*

O MY JESUS, forgive us our sins, save us from the fires of Hell, lead all souls to Heaven, especially those who are most in need of Thy mercy.

— End of the Five Fatima Prayers —

How to Pray the Rosary

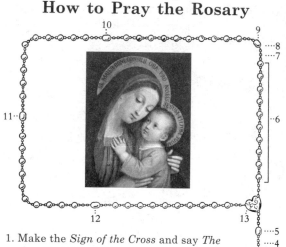

1. Make the *Sign of the Cross* and say *The Apostles' Creed.*
2. Say the *Our Father.*
3. Say 3 *Hail Mary's.*
4. Say the *Glory be to the Father.*
5. Announce the First Mystery; then say the *Our Father.*
6. Say 10 *Hail Mary's.*
7. Say the *Glory be to the Father.*
8. Say the *O My Jesus.*
9. Announce the Second Mystery; then say the *Our Father*, 10 *Hail Mary's, Glory be* and *O My Jesus.*
10. Announce the Third Mystery; then say the *Our Father*, 10 *Hail Mary's, Glory be* and *O My Jesus.*
11. Announce the Fourth Mystery; then say the *Our Father*, 10 *Hail Mary's, Glory be* and *O My Jesus.*
12. Announce the Fifth Mystery; then say the *Our Father,*

10 *Hail Marys, Glory be* and *O My Jesus.*
13. Conclude by saying the *Hail, Holy Queen.*
14. Follow with *Prayer After the Rosary,* if desired. (See opposite page.)

The Mysteries of the Rosary
To be meditated upon while praying the Rosary.
(The classic 15 Mysteries given by Our Lady to St. Dominic.)

THE JOYFUL MYSTERIES
Said on Mondays and Thursdays and the Sundays from the First Sunday of Advent until Lent.

1st Joyful Mystery: The Annunciation
2nd Joyful Mystery: The Visitation
3rd Joyful Mystery: The Nativity
4th Joyful Mystery: The Presentation of Our Lord in the Temple
5th Joyful Mystery: The Finding of Our Lord in the Temple

THE SORROWFUL MYSTERIES
Said on Tuesdays and Fridays and daily during Lent.

1st Sorrowful Mystery: The Agony in the Garden
2nd Sorrowful Mystery: The Scourging at the Pillar
3rd Sorrowful Mystery: The Crowning with Thorns
4th Sorrowful Mystery: The Carrying of the Cross
5th Sorrowful Mystery: The Crucifixion and Death of Our Lord on the Cross

THE GLORIOUS MYSTERIES
Said on Wednesdays and Saturdays and the Sundays from Easter until Advent.

1st Glorious Mystery: The Resurrection of Our Lord
2nd Glorious Mystery: The Ascension of Our Lord
3rd Glorious Mystery: The Descent of the Holy Ghost upon the Apostles

4th Glorious Mystery: The Assumption of the Blessed
                      Virgin Mary into Heaven
5th Glorious Mystery: The Coronation of Our Lady as
                      Queen of Heaven and Earth

THE LUMINOUS MYSTERIES*
*Said on Thursdays, with Saturday being changed to
a day for praying the Joyful Mysteries.*

1st Luminous Mystery: The Baptism in the Jordan
2nd Luminous Mystery: Our Lord's Self-manifestation
                      at the Wedding of Cana
3rd Luminous Mystery: The proclamation of the
                      Kingdom of God and call to
                      conversion
4th Luminous Mystery: The Transfiguration
5th Luminous Mystery: The Institution of the Eucharist,
                      as the sacramental expression
                      of the Paschal Mystery

* *Publisher's Note: The Luminous Mysteries were added to this
book in 2008 as required by Most Reverend Thomas G. Doran,
Ordinary of the Diocese of Rockford, as a condition for granting the Imprimatur. The Luminous Mysteries were introduced
by Pope John Paul II in 2002 as an optional addition to the
traditional Rosary.*

Prayer after the Rosary

O GOD, Whose only-begotten Son, by His
life, death and Resurrection, has purchased for us the rewards of eternal salvation, grant, we beseech Thee, that,
meditating upon these Mysteries of the
Most Holy Rosary of the Blessed Virgin
Mary, we may both imitate what they contain and obtain what they promise. Through
the same Christ Our Lord. Amen.

Prayer for the Seven Gifts
Of the Holy Ghost

O LORD JESUS CHRIST, Who before ascending into Heaven didst promise to send the Holy Ghost to finish Thy work in the souls of Thine Apostles and Disciples, deign to grant the same Holy Spirit to me, that He may perfect in my soul the work of Thy grace and Thy love. Grant me the spirit of wisdom, that I may despise the perishable things of this world and aspire only after the things that are eternal; the spirit of understanding, to enlighten my mind with the light of Thy divine truth; the spirit of counsel, that I may ever choose the surest way of pleasing God and gaining Heaven; the spirit of fortitude, that I may bear my cross with Thee and that I may overcome with courage all the obstacles that oppose my salvation; the spirit of knowledge, that I may know God and know myself and grow perfect in the science of the Saints; the spirit of piety, that I may find the service of God sweet and amiable; the spirit of fear, that I may be filled with a loving reverence

81

towards God and may dread in any way to displease Him. Mark me, dear Lord, with the sign of Thy true disciples, and animate me in all things with Thy Spirit. Amen.

Prayer for Direction in the Choice of a State of Life

O ALMIGHTY GOD, Whose wise and amiable providence watches over every human event, be Thou my light and my counsel in all my undertakings, particularly in the choice of a state of life. I know that on this important step my sanctification and salvation in great measure depend. I know that I am incapable of discerning what may be best for me; therefore, I cast myself into Thy arms, beseeching Thee, my God, Who hast sent me into this world only to know, love and serve Thee, to direct by Thy grace every moment and action of my life to the glorious end of my creation. I renounce most sincerely every other wish than to fulfill Thy designs on my soul, whatever they may be, and I beseech Thee to grant me that grace which, by imbibing the true spirit of a Christian, will enable me to qualify myself for any state of life to which Thine adorable Providence may call me. O my God, whenever it may become my duty to make a choice, do Thou be my Light and my Counsel, and mercifully *make known to me the way wherein I should walk, for I have lifted up my soul to Thee.* Preserve me from listening to the suggestions of my own self-love, or worldly prudence, in prejudice to Thy holy inspirations. Let *Thy good Spirit lead me into the right way*, and let Thine adorable providence place me, not where I may naturally feel inclined to go, but where all things may be most conducive to Thy glory and to the good of my soul.

Mary, Mother of Good Counsel, Seat of Wisdom and Help of Christians, pray for me.

A Prayer for Priests

O JESUS, Eternal Priest, keep all Thy priests within the shelter of Thy Sacred Heart, where none may harm them.

Keep unstained their anointed hands, which daily touch Thy Sacred Body. Keep unsullied their lips purpled with Thy Precious Blood.

Keep pure and unearthly their hearts sealed with the sublime marks of Thy glorious priesthood.

Let Thy holy love surround them and shield them from the world's contagion.

Bless their labors with abundant fruit,

and may the souls to whom they have ministered here below be their joy and consolation and in Heaven their beautiful and everlasting crown. Amen.

O Mary, Queen of the clergy, pray for us, and obtain for us a number of holy priests.

Prayer to Our Lady of Guadalupe For the Conversion of the Americas and of the World

O HOLY MARY, Virgin Mother of God, who as Our Lady of Guadalupe didst aid in the conversion of Mexico from paganism in a most miraculous way, we now beseech thee to bring about in these our times the early conversion of our modern world from its present neo-paganism to the One, Holy, Catholic and Apostolic Church of thy divine Son, Jesus Christ, starting in the Americas and extending throughout the entire world, so that soon there may be truly "one fold and one shepherd," with all governments recognizing the reign of thy Son, Jesus Christ the King. This we ask of the Eternal Father, through Jesus Christ His Son Our Lord and by thy powerful intercession—all for the salvation of souls, the triumph of the Church and peace in the world. Amen.

A Morning Offering
By St. Therese of Lisieux

O MY GOD! I offer Thee all my actions of this day for the intentions and for the glory of the Sacred Heart of Jesus. I desire to sanctify every beat of my heart, my every thought, my simplest works, by uniting them to Its infinite merits; and I wish to make reparation for my sins by casting them into the furnace of Its Merciful Love.

O my God! I ask of Thee for myself and for those whom I hold dear, the grace to fulfill perfectly Thy Holy Will, to accept for love of Thee the joys and sorrows of this passing life, so that we may one day be united together in Heaven for all Eternity. Amen.

Novena Rose Prayer

O LITTLE Therese of the Child Jesus, please pick for me a rose from the heavenly gardens and send it to me as a message of love.

O LITTLE Flower of Jesus, ask God today to grant the favors I now place with confidence in your hands . . . (*Mention your requests*).

ST. THERESE, help me to always believe, as you did, in God's great love for me, so that I might imitate your "Little Way" each day. Amen.

Prayer to Our Lady Of Mental Peace

O MOTHER of tranquility, Mother of hope, Our Lady of Mental Peace, we reach out to thee for what is needful in our weakness. Teach a searching heart that God's love is unchanging, that human love begins and grows by touching His Love.

Our Lady of Mental Peace, pray for us!

Night Prayer for Daily Neglects

ETERNAL FATHER, I offer Thee the Sacred Heart of Jesus, with all its love, all its sufferings and all its merits . . .

To expiate all the sins I have committed this day and during all my life.

Glory Be . . .

Eternal Father . . . *(Repeat the beginning prayer.)*

To purify the good I have done badly this day and during all my life.

Glory Be . . .

Eternal Father . . . *(Repeat the beginning prayer.)*

To supply for the good I ought to have done and that I have neglected this day and during all my life.

Glory Be . . .

Prayer for Detachment From Earthly Goods

O JESUS, Who didst choose a life of poverty and obscurity, grant me the grace to keep my heart detached from the transitory things of this world. Be Thou henceforth my only treasure, for Thou art infinitely more precious than all other possessions. My heart is too solicitous for the vain and fleeting things of earth. Make me always mindful of Thy warning words: "What does it profit a man if he gain the whole world, but suffer the loss of his own soul?" Grant me the grace to keep Thy holy example always before my eyes, that I may despise the nothingness of this world and make Thee the object of all my desires and affections. Amen.

Prayer to St. Joseph
For Purity

O GUARDIAN of virgins and holy father St. Joseph, into whose faithful custody Christ Jesus, Innocence Itself, and Mary, Virgin of virgins, were committed, I pray and beseech thee, by these dear pledges, Jesus and Mary, that being preserved from all impurity, I may with spotless mind, pure heart and chaste body ever most chastely serve Jesus and Mary all the days of my life. Amen.

Prayer to St. Aloysius
For Purity

SAINT ALOYSIUS, adorned with angelic virtues, I commend to thee most earnestly the chastity of my mind and body. I pray thee, by thine angelic purity, to commend me to the Immaculate Lamb, Jesus Christ, and to His most holy Mother, the Virgin of virgins, and to protect me from every grievous sin. Permit me not to defile myself by any spot of impurity; and when thou seest me in temptation or in danger of sin, banish far from my heart every unclean thought and desire. Awaken in me the thought of eternity and of Jesus Crucified;

imprint deeply in my heart a lively sense of the holy fear of God; set me on fire with the love of God, and grant me the grace to imitate thee on earth, that I may enjoy the possession of God with thee in Heaven. Amen.

Prayer to Overcome Sloth And Lukewarmness

O MY GOD, I know well that so negligent a life as mine cannot please Thee. I know that by my lukewarmness I have closed the door to the graces which Thou dost desire to bestow upon me. O my God, do not reject me, as I deserve, but continue to be merciful toward me, and I will make great efforts to amend and to arise from this miserable state. In the future I will be more careful to overcome my passions, to follow Thine inspirations, and never through slothfulness will I omit my duties, but will ever strive to fulfill them with greater diligence and fidelity. In short, I will from this time forward do all I can to please Thee and will neglect nothing which I know to be pleasing to Thee.

Since Thou, O my Jesus, hast been so liberal with Thy graces toward me and hast deigned to give Thy Blood and Thy Life for me, I am sorry for having acted with so little generosity toward Thee, Who art worthy of all honor and all love. But O my Jesus, Thou knowest my weakness. Help me with Thy powerful grace; in Thee I confide. O Immaculate Virgin Mary, help me to overcome myself and to become a Saint. Amen.

Prayer to Overcome Bad Habits

BEHOLD me, O my God, at Thy feet! I do not deserve mercy, but O, my Redeemer, the blood which Thou hast shed for me encourages me and obliges me to hope for it. How often have I offended Thee, repented, and yet have I again fallen into the same sin.

O my God, I wish to amend, and in order to be faithful to Thee, I will place all my confidence in Thee. I will, whenever I am tempted, instantly have recourse to Thee. Hitherto, I have trusted in my own promises and resolutions and have neglected to recommend myself to Thee in my temptations. This has been the cause of my repeated failures. From this day forward, be Thou, O Lord, my strength, and thus shall I be able to do all things, for "I can do all things in Him who strengtheneth me." Amen.

Prayer to Overcome a Vice

O GOD, who didst break the chains of blessed Peter the Apostle and didst make him come forth from prison unscathed, loose the bonds of Thy servant, (*Name*), held in captivity by the vice of _____, and by the merits of the same Apostle, do Thou grant me (*him, her*) to be delivered from its tyranny. Remove from my (*his, her*) heart all excessive love of sensual pleasures and gratifications, so that living soberly, justly and piously, I (*he, she*) may attain to everlasting life with Thee. Amen.

Prayer Against Evil Thoughts

A LMIGHTY and merciful God, look favorably upon my prayer and free my heart from temptation to evil thoughts, that I may deserve to be accounted a worthy dwelling place of the Holy Spirit. Shed upon my heart the brightness of Thy grace, that I may ever think thoughts worthy of Thy Divine Majesty and that are pleasing to Thee, and ever sincerely love Thee, through Christ Our Lord. Amen.

A Prayer for Grace

O MY GOD, remember that moment when, for the first time, Thou didst pour Thy grace into my soul, washing me from Original Sin, that Thou might receive me into the number of Thy children. O God, Thou Who art my Father, grant me in Thine infinite mercy, through the merits and the Blood of Jesus Christ and through the sorrows of the Holy Virgin Mary, the graces which Thou dost desire that I should receive this day for Thy greater glory and my salvation. Amen.

O Heart of Love, I place all my trust in Thee, for though I fear all things from my own weakness, I hope all things from Thy goodness.

O purest Heart of the Blessed Virgin Mary, obtain for me from Jesus a pure and humble heart. Amen.

Prayer to St. Joseph
For a Happy Death

O GLORIOUS ST. JOSEPH, behold I choose thee today for my special patron in life and at the hour of my death. Preserve and increase in me the spirit of prayer and fervor in the service of God.

Remove far from me every kind of sin, and obtain for me that my death may not come upon me unawares, but that I may have time to confess my sins sacramentally and to bewail them with a most perfect understanding and a most sincere contrition, in order that I may breathe forth my soul into the hands of Jesus and Mary. Amen.

Acceptance of Death

O LORD GOD, I look ahead to the end of my life, and with true contrition for having offended Thee, I accept in advance, from Thy loving hands, whatever death it will please Thee to send me. I accept this death with all its pains, anguish and suffering, in reparation for my sins and for love of Thee. I rely on Thine all-powerful grace to see me through my last hours, moment by moment, and to bring me home to a happy eternity with Thee forever. Through Jesus Christ Our Lord. Amen.

O Mary, Mother of departing souls, pray for us.

St. Joseph, Patron of a Happy Death, pray for us.

Prayer for
Those in Their Agony

O MOST merciful Jesus, lover of souls, I beseech Thee, by the agony of Thy most Sacred Heart and by the sorrows of Thine Immaculate Mother, cleanse in Thine own blood the sinners of the whole world who are now in their agony and are to die this day. Amen.

Heart of Jesus, Most Merciful Saviour, who was once in the agony of death, have pity on the dying. Amen.

Prayer to Our Lord on
The Cross for a Happy Hour
Of Death

O MY crucified Jesus, mercifully accept the prayer which I now make to Thee for help in the moment of my death, when at its approach all my senses shall fail me.

When, therefore, O sweetest Jesus, my weary and downcast eyes can no longer look up to Thee, be mindful of the loving gaze which now I turn on Thee, and have mercy on me.

When my parched lips can no longer kiss Thy most sacred Wounds, remember then those kisses which now I imprint on Thee, and have mercy on me.

When my cold hands can no longer embrace Thy Cross, forget not the affection with which I embrace it now, and have mercy on me.

And when, at length, my swollen and lifeless tongue can no longer speak, remember that I called upon Thee now.

Jesus, Mary, Joseph, to Thee do I commend my soul.

Prayer for a Deceased Person

O GOD, Whose way it is always to have mercy and to spare, we beseech Thee on behalf of the soul of Thy servant (*Name*), whom Thou hast called out of this world: look upon him (*her*) with pity and let him be conducted by the holy Angels to Paradise, his true country. Grant that he who believed in Thee and hoped in Thee may not be left to suffer the pains of the Purgatorial fire, but may be admitted to eternal joys, through Jesus Christ, Thy Son Our Lord, who with Thee and the Holy Ghost, liveth and reigneth world without end. Amen.

Our Father, Hail Mary, Glory Be.

V. Eternal rest grant unto him (*her*), O Lord;

R. *And let perpetual light shine upon him (her).*

V. May he (*she*) rest in peace.

R. *Amen.*

Prayer for the Poor Souls

O MOST gentle Heart of Jesus, ever present in the Blessed Sacrament, ever consumed with burning love for the poor captive souls in Purgatory, have mercy on the souls of Thy departed servants. Be not severe in Thy judgments, but let some drops of Thy Precious Blood fall upon the devouring flames. And do Thou, O Merciful Saviour, send Thy holy Angels to conduct them to a place of refreshment, light and peace. Amen.

A Prayer for the Dead

O GOD, the Creator and Redeemer of all the Faithful, grant unto the souls of Thy departed servants full remission of all their sins, that through the help of our pious supplications they may obtain that pardon which they have always desired, Thou Who livest and reignest world without end. Amen.

V. Eternal rest grant unto them, O Lord.

R. *And let perpetual light shine upon them.*
V. May the divine assistance remain always
with us. Amen.
R. *And may the souls of all the Faithful
departed, through the mercy of God, rest
in peace. Amen.*

A Prayer for
Our Dear Departed

O GOOD JESUS, Whose loving Heart
was ever troubled by the sorrows of
others, look with pity on the souls of our
dear ones in Purgatory, especially (*Names*).
O Thou Who didst "love Thine own," hear
our cry for mercy, and grant that those
whom Thou hast called from our homes and
hearts may soon enjoy everlasting rest in
the home of Thy Love in Heaven. Amen.

V. Eternal rest grant unto them, O Lord.
R. *And let perpetual light shine upon them.
Amen.*

Prayer to St. Peregrine
"The Cancer Saint"

O GLORIOUS wonder-worker, St. Peregrine, who suffered so patiently with
incurable cancer in thy leg and then wert
healed miraculously by a touch of Our

Lord's divine hand, I beg of thee to obtain for me deliverance from the infirmities that afflict my body (*especially . . .*), if this be God's Holy Will. Obtain for me also a perfect resignation to the sufferings it may please God to send me, so that, imitating our crucified Saviour and His sorrowful Mother, I may merit eternal glory in Heaven. Amen.

St. Peregrine, pray for us.

Prayer to St. Gerard
For Motherhood

O GOOD St. Gerard, powerful patron and protector of mothers and of children yet unborn, to thee do I turn in my hour of anxiety. Of thee do I beg the blessings of a happy motherhood. When all human assistance seems to fail, deign to come to my aid by thy powerful intercession at the throne of Almighty God. Beseech the Divine Author of Life to bless me with offspring, that I may raise up children to God in this life who will be heirs to His heavenly Kingdom in the next. Amen.

Prayer to St. Gerard
For a Mother with Child
(To be said either for oneself or for another.)

O ALMIGHTY and Everlasting God, Who through the operation of the Holy Ghost didst prepare the body and soul of the glorious Virgin Mary to be a worthy dwelling place of Thy Divine Son; and through the operation of the same Holy Ghost, didst sanctify St. John the Baptist while still in his mother's womb, hearken to the prayers of Thy humble servant who implores Thee, through the intercession of St. Gerard, to protect her (*me*) amidst the dangers of childbearing and to watch over the child with which Thou hast deigned to bless her (*me*): that it may be cleansed by the saving water of Baptism, and that, after living a Christian life on earth, both the child and its mother may attain to everlasting bliss in Heaven. Amen.

Prayer to St. Gerard in
Thanksgiving for
A Safe Delivery

O GOOD St. Gerard, wonderful Patron of Mothers, deign to offer to God my heartfelt gratitude for the great blessing of motherhood. In my long hours of anxiety, uncertainty and doubt, thy powerful intercession with Jesus my Lord and Mary my Queen was ever my hope. Obtain for me the grace always to turn to thee in similar trials. Help me to inspire other women with confidence in thy most gracious assistance. Aid all of us, that, doing God's holy Will as mothers here on earth, we may merit eternal life in Heaven, through Jesus Christ Our Lord. Amen.

Prayer in Honor of St. Dymphna, Patroness of Those with Mental And Nervous Disorders

O LORD GOD, Who has graciously chosen St. Dymphna to be the patroness of those afflicted with mental and nervous disorders and has caused her to be an inspiration and a symbol of charity to the thousands who invoke her intercession, grant, through the prayers of this pure, youthful martyr, relief and consolation to all who suffer from these disturbances, and especially to those for whom we now pray. (*Here mention oneself or names of others*.)

We beg Thee to accept and to satisfy the prayers of St. Dymphna on our behalf. Grant us patience in all our sufferings and resignation to Thy divine Will. Fill us with hope, and if it be in accord with Thy divine plan, bestow upon me (him, her) the cure I so earnestly ask for. Through Christ Our Lord. Amen.

Novena Prayer to the Infant Jesus of Prague For a Special Favor

O DEAREST JESUS, tenderly loving us, Thy greatest joy is to dwell among us and to bestow Thy blessing upon us! Though I am not worthy that Thou shouldst behold me with love, I feel myself drawn to Thee, O dear Infant Jesus, because Thou dost gladly pardon me and exercise Thine almighty power over me.

So many who turned with confidence to Thee have received graces and had their petitions granted. Behold me: in spirit I kneel before Thy miraculous image on Thine altar in Prague and lay open my heart to Thee, with its prayers, petitions and hopes. Especially the affair of *(Name your request)* do I enclose in Thy loving Heart. Govern me and do with me and mine according to Thy holy will, for I know that in Thy Divine wisdom and love Thou wilt ordain everything for the best. Almighty gracious Infant Jesus, do not withdraw Thy hand from us, but protect and bless us forever.

I pray Thee, sweetest Infant, in the name of Thy Blessed Mother Mary, who cared for Thee with such tenderness, and by the great reverence with which St. Joseph carried Thee in his arms, comfort me and grant my petition, that I may bless and thank Thee forever with all my heart. Amen.

Prayer of a Sick Person for Health of Body and Soul

This prayer can be prayed by anyone. It includes acts of faith, love and perfect contrition.

O LORD Jesus Christ, Who during Thy brief life on earth went about doing good to all men, be merciful to me in this, my hour of special need.

O Divine Physician, Thy tender heart was ever moved at the sight of pain and affliction. I beg of Thee, if it be Thy holy Will, to help me regain my health and strength. Stretch forth Thy hand to all who suffer, whether in mind or in body. Grant to each of us that peace of soul which Thou alone canst give.

I believe that in God there are three Divine Persons—Father, Son, and Holy Spirit.

I believe that God so loved the world that He sent Thee, His only-begotten Son, Who died on the Cross for our salvation.

I believe that God, in His mercy and justice, rewards goodness and punishes evil.

I am truly sorry for all my sins, Dear Lord, because they have offended Thee, Who art Goodness itself. I love Thee with all my heart, and with Thy help, I will try never to offend Thee again. Assist me to do all that is necessary to obtain eternal life.

Jesus, Son of David, have mercy on me!

Prayer in Time of Sickness

O DIVINE PHYSICIAN, Who always loved to console and heal the sick of body and mind, grant me patience to bear my sufferings. By Thy power, relieve the sharpness of my pain and exhaustion, but above all, kind Jesus, heal the wounds of my soul. And even though I find it hard to pray, yet shall I ever say: Thy Will be done. Amen.

Prayer to St. Maria Goretti for Purity and Holiness

O ST. MARIA GORETTI, strengthened by God's grace, thou didst not hesitate, even at the age of eleven, to sacrifice life itself to defend thy virginal purity. Look graciously on the unhappy human race that has strayed far from the path of eternal salvation. Teach us that promptness in fleeing temptation that will help us avoid anything that could offend Jesus. Obtain for me a great horror of impurity and of all sin, so that I may live a holy life on earth and win eternal glory in Heaven. Amen.

Our Father, Hail Mary, Glory Be.

A Child's Prayer through the Intercession of St. John Bosco

O ALMIGHTY GOD, Who hast given me my father and mother and made them an image of Thine authority and love, and hast commanded me to love, honor and obey them: grant me, through the intercession of St. John Bosco, grace to observe faithfully this law. Grant me grace to profit from their admonitions, and make me respect all those who take their place. Deliver me from pride, rebellion, stubbornness, evil temper and laziness. Make me diligent in all my duties and patient in all my trials, so that one day I may be happy with Thee forever in Heaven. Amen.

Prayer to
St. Anthony Mary Claret
For the Cure of Cancer or
Other Serious Ailment

Our Lady told St. Anthony Mary Claret (1807-1870) that she would obtain from God anything he asked for through her Immaculate Heart.

O ST. ANTHONY MARY CLARET, who during thy life on earth was often a solace to the afflicted, and didst love and tenderly compassionate the sick, intercede for me as thou dost rejoice in the reward of thy virtues. Cast a glance of pity on *(here mention the person afflicted with cancer or other serious ailment)* and grant my petition, if such be the will of God. Make my troubles thine own. Ask the Immaculate Heart of Mary to obtain by her powerful intercession the grace I yearn for so ardently, and a blessing that may strengthen me during life, assist me at the hour of death and lead me on to a happy eternity. Amen.

St. Anthony Mary Claret, pray for us!

Our Father, Hail Mary, Glory Be.

Prayer to St. Raphael
The Archangel for a Cure

O GOOD St. Raphael, I invoke thee as the patron of those who are afflicted with bodily illness or ailment. Thou didst prepare the remedy which cured the blindness of the elder Tobias, and thy name means "God has healed."

I turn to thee for help in my present need. (*Mention your request.*) If it be the Will of God, deign to cure my ailment, or at least to give me the strength I need to bear it patiently in atonement for my sins and for the salvation of my soul. Teach me to unite my sufferings with those of Jesus and Mary and to seek God's grace in prayer and Holy Communion. I wish to imitate thee in thy zeal to do God's Will in all things. Like young Tobias, I choose thee as my companion on my journey through this valley of tears. I wish to follow thine inspirations every step of the way, so that I may reach my journey's end under thy constant protection and in the grace of God.

St. Raphael, to the elder Tobias thou didst reveal thyself as "the help of the grace of God." Be thou my help and deign to obtain for me the grace of God and the favor I ask of thee through thy powerful intercession.

Physician from God, deign to cure me as thou didst cure Tobias.

St. Raphael, thou who art called "the Remedy of God" and "the Angel of Health," pray for me. Amen.

In honor of St. Raphael, recite one Our Father, Hail Mary and Glory Be.

Prayer to St. Raphael
For the Wise Choice of a Marriage Partner

O GLORIOUS St. Raphael, Patron and Lover of the Young, I call upon thee and plead with thee for thy help. In all confidence I open my heart to thee, to beg thy guidance and assistance in the important task of planning my future. Obtain for me through thy intercession the light of God's grace, so that I may decide wisely concerning the person who is to be my partner through life. O Angel of Happy Meetings, lead us by the hand to find each other. May all our movements be guided by thy light and transfigured by thy joy. As thou didst lead the young Tobias to Sara and opened up for him a new life of happiness with her in holy marriage, lead me to such a one whom in thine angelic wisdom thou dost judge best suited to be united with me in marriage.

St. Raphael, loving Patron of those seeking a marriage partner, help me in this supreme decision of my life. Find for me as a helpmate in life that person whose character will reflect the traits of Jesus and Mary. May he (*she*) be upright, loyal, pure, sincere and noble, so that with united efforts and with chaste and unselfish love, we both may strive to perfect ourselves in soul and body, as well as the children it may please God to entrust to our care.

St. Raphael, Angel of chaste courtship, bless our friendship and our love, that sin may have no part in it. May our mutual love bind us so closely that our future home may ever be most like the home of the Holy Family of Nazareth. Offer thy prayers to God for both of us and obtain the blessing of God upon our marriage, as thou wert the herald of blessing for the marriage of Tobias and Sara.

St. Raphael, Friend of the Young, be thou my friend, for I shall always be thine. I desire ever to invoke thee in my needs. To thy special care I entrust the decision I am to make as to my future wife (*husband*). Direct me to the person with whom I can best cooperate in doing God's Holy Will, with whom I can live in peace, love and harmony in this life and attain to eternal joy in the next. Amen.

In honor of Saint Raphael recite one Our Father, Hail Mary and Glory Be.

Prayer to St. Raphael
For Purity

ST. RAPHAEL, Patron Angel of Youth, I beg of thee to plead with God for me, that I may always keep my life pure and holy. As thou didst guard the young Tobias from dangers of soul and body on his journey to a strange land, protect me from the many dangers that confront me in my life. Strengthen me in my struggle against the temptations of the world, the flesh and the devil.

I pray and beg of thee, glorious St. Raphael, to be my Patron Angel of Purity. For thy great love for Jesus, the King of the Angels, and for Mary, the Queen of the Angels, deign to keep me from all uncleanness and to obtain that my mind may be untainted, my heart pure and my body chaste. May I frequently receive the "Bread of Angels" in Holy Communion, that It may be an effective remedy and protection against the temptations that press round

about me, and seal my heart forever against
the suggestions of sinful pleasures. Help me
always to serve Jesus and Mary in perfect
chastity, so that one day I may merit to
belong to those of whom Jesus spoke when
He said, "Blessed are the pure of heart, for
they shall see God." Amen.

Prayer to Our Sorrowful Mother for a Favor

MOST holy and afflicted Virgin, Queen of
Martyrs, who stood beneath the
Cross, witnessing the agony of thy dying
Son, look with a mother's tenderness and
pity on me, who kneel before thee. To whom
shall I have recourse in my needs and miseries if not to thee, O Mother of Mercy?
Thou hast drunk so deeply of the chalice of
thy Son that thou canst compassionate all
our sorrows. I venerate thy sorrows, and I
place my request with filial confidence in
the sanctuary of thy wounded heart. (*Here
mention your request.*)

Present it, I beseech thee, on my behalf to
Jesus Christ, through the merits of His own
most sacred Passion and Death, together
with thine own sufferings at the foot of the
Cross. Through the united efficacy of both

thy Son's sufferings and thy own, obtain the granting of my petition.

Holy Mary, whose soul was pierced by a sword of sorrow at the sight of the Passion of thy divine Son, intercede for me and obtain for me from Jesus this favor, if it be for His honor and glory and for my good. Amen.

Prayer for a Person Who is Seriously Ill

MOST merciful Jesus, the Consolation and Salvation of all who put their trust in Thee, we humbly beseech Thee, by Thy most bitter Passion, grant recovery of health to Thy servant (*Name*), provided this be for his (*her*) soul's welfare, that with us he (*she*) may praise and magnify Thy holy name. But if it be Thy holy will to call him (*her*) out of this world, strengthen him (*her*) in his (*her*) last hour, grant him (*her*) a peaceful death and bring him (*her*) to life everlasting. Amen.

Our Father, Hail Mary, Glory Be.

Novena Prayer to Our Mother Of Perpetual Help

O MOTHER of Perpetual Help, thou art the dispenser of all the gifts which God grants to us miserable sinners; and for this end He has made thee so powerful, so rich and so bountiful, in order that thou mayest help us in our misery. Thou art the advocate of the most wretched and abandoned sinners who have recourse to thee. Come to my aid, dearest Mother, for I recommend myself to thee. In thy hands I place my eternal salvation, and to thee do I entrust my soul. Count me among thy most devoted servants; take me under thy protection, and it is enough for me. For if thou wilt protect me, dear Mother, I fear nothing: not from my sins, because thou wilt obtain for me the pardon of them; nor from the devils, because thou art more powerful than all Hell together; nor even from Jesus, my Judge Himself, because by one prayer from thee, He will be appeased. But one thing I fear, that in the hour of temptation, I may neglect to call upon thee and thus perish miserably.

Obtain for me, then, O Mother of Perpetual Help, the pardon of my sins, love for Jesus, final perseverance, and the grace to have recourse to thee always.

Three Hail Marys.

A Prayer to Our Mother
Of Perpetual Help for
The Conversion of a Sinner

O MARY, Mother of Perpetual Help, thou knowest so well the great value of an immortal soul. Thou knowest what it means, that every soul has been redeemed by the Blood of thy Divine Son. Thou wilt not then despise my prayer if I ask from thee the conversion of a sinner, nay, a great sinner, who is rapidly hurrying on toward eternal ruin. Thou, O good and merciful Mother, knowest well his (*her*) irregular life. Remember that thou art the Refuge of Sinners; remember that God has given thee power to bring about the conversion of even the most wretched sinners. All that has been done for his (*her*) soul has been unsuccessful; if thou wilt not come to his (*her*) assistance, he (*she*) will go from bad to worse. Obtain for him (*her*) the effectual grace that he (*she*) may be moved and brought back to God and to his (*her*) duties. Send him (*her*), if necessary, temporal calamities and trials, that he (*she*) may enter into himself (*herself*) and put an end to his (*her*) sinful course. Thou, O most merciful Mother, hast converted so many sinners through thine intercession, at the prayer to thee of their friends. Be then also moved by *my* prayer, and bring this unhappy soul to true conversion of heart.

O Mother of Perpetual Help, deign to show that thou art the Advocate and Refuge of Sinners. So I hope, so may it be. Amen.

Deliver Us From Evil

The prayer Libera Nos *is said after the Pater Noster of the Traditional Mass.*

DELIVER us, we beseech Thee, O Lord, from all evils, past, present and to come, and by the intercession of the blessed and glorious Mary ever virgin, Mother of God, and of Thy blessed Apostles Peter and Paul, and of Andrew and of all Thy Saints, mercifully grant peace in our days, that aided by the help of Thy mercy, we may be always free from sin and secure from all disturbance, through the same Jesus Christ, Thy Son, our Lord, Who lives and reigns with Thee in the unity of the Holy Spirit, one God, for ever and ever. Amen.